Blue-Tongued Skir

CW01498328

Blue-Tongued Skink Facts

Blue-Tongued Skink Care, Behavior, Diet, Interaction, Costs and Health.

By

Ben Team

Table of Contents

Table of Contents...3

Foreword 5

About the Author 8

PART I: THE BLUE-TONGUED SKINK 9

Chapter 1: Blue-Tongued Skink Description and Anatomy 10

Chapter 2: Blue-Tongued Skink Biology and Behavior 15

Chapter 3: Classification and Taxonomy 19

Chapter 4: The Blue-Tongued Skink's World 20

PART II: BLUE-TONGUED SKINK HUSBANDRY 24

Chapter 5: Blue-Tongued Skinks as Pets................................... 25

Chapter 6: Providing the Captive Habitat 38

Chapter 7: Heating the Habitat 44

Chapter 8: Lighting the Enclosure... 56

Chapter 9: Enclosure Furniture 59

Chapter 10: Substrates.. 64

Chapter 11: Maintaining the Captive Habitat 67

Chapter 12: Feeding Blue-Tongued Skinks 73

Chapter 13: Providing Water to Your Blue-Tongued Skink 80

Chapter 14: Interacting with Your Blue-Tongued Skink 82

Chapter 15: Common Health Concerns 86

Chapter 16: Breeding Blue-Tongued Skinks................................. 96

Chapter 17: Further Reading **101**

References **107**

Foreword

Although there are some exceptions, sedentary reptiles often make much better pets than their widely ranging, actively foraging counterparts do.

For a variety of reasons, the species in the former category are simply better suited for captive life, and they're generally more fun to care for than those in the latter category.

For example, highly active species usually require much more space than those who sit around and wait for food to come to them. Consider that a 4-foot-long ball python may only need 6 to 8 square feet of space to live a long, healthy life, but a 4-foot-long black racer would need an enclosure at least twice this size to feel comfortable.

Additionally, most reptiles who are very active are also quite defensive, and they rarely appreciate interacting with their keepers. They'll wiggle and squirm when held, usually while biting and releasing copious quantities of musk in the process.

By contrast, many (although certainly not all) low-activity species tolerate gentle, occasional and brief interactions with their keepers.

Snakes, lizards and turtles who tend to move around a lot also tend to require more maintenance, as they typically eat and defecate frequently. They also cause more wear-and-tear on the habitat and furniture contained inside.

Given these facts, it shouldn't be surprising that blue-tongued skinks – some of the more sedentary lizards in the world – often make excellent pets.

Most blue-tongued skinks spend their lives living in relatively small areas, and they tend to avoid traveling long distances or crossing open, exposed areas whenever possible.

They don't even run when they're threatened; they stand their ground and initiate a startling defensive display, which they're prepared to follow with a strong bite if need be.

In fact, some blue-tongued skink populations manage to survive in suburban areas – even when most other lizards and snakes have been extirpated. They maintain a low-profile lifestyle, subsist on the types of foods that are common in these areas, and don't cause any problems for the humans living alongside them.

In light of this, it seems obvious that blue-tongued skinks would thrive in captivity.

***

There are actually a number of different species and subspecies of blue-tongued skink, and each has adapted to the environment and food-web that is characteristic of the area. But, while some species and subspecies may require slightly higher temperatures or slightly more space than others, they all thrive under relatively similar husbandry regimens.

Fortunately for those who wish to keep these unique lizards, their husbandry requirements are often very simple to satisfy. Over time, keepers have devised a relatively straightforward "formula" for keeping these lizards healthy, and many keepers have even had success breeding these lizards in captivity. In fact, they're quite common in the marketplace and readily available.

And despite their willingness to stand up to threats in the wild, captive blue-tongued skinks – particularly captive-bred animals – are usually quite calm and docile. In fact, some keepers believe that their blue-tongued skink actually likes gentle interaction. This seems like quite the anthropomorphism, and it is difficult to be certain, but, at the very least, it illustrates the fact that these lizards often tolerate handling quite well.

Given their ease of care and laid-back personalities, blue-tongued skinks make great pets for beginning reptile keepers. They'll rarely act antagonistically or present difficult husbandry challenges, and they're relatively well-known by a large swath of those in the reptile-keeping hobby, so it is generally easy to find information about these interesting lizards.

***

Nevertheless, while blue-tongued skinks are generally easy to care for and they are usually well-behaved pets, you'll still have to learn all you can about their lifestyle, biology and behavior before you add one to your home.

Fail to do so and you'll likely struggle to keep your lizard healthy, and he'll ultimately suffer a premature death. We'll help you start this process on the following pages, as we discuss the most important issues potential blue-tongued skink keepers should understand.

But don't consider this to be the end of your journey. Learning about your lizard will be a long-term process, and you'll want to continue to read as much as you can for the entire time you care for your pet. So, be sure to check out Chapter 17: "Further Reading" once you understand the basics.

With a little bit of effort and research, you should find your new blue-tongued skink easy to care for, and you'll probably find him to be a very rewarding pet.

About the Author

The author, Ben Team, is an environmental educator and author with over 16 years of professional reptile-keeping experience.

Ben currently maintains www.FootstepsInTheForest.com, where he shares information, narration and observations of the natural world.

PART I: THE BLUE-TONGUED SKINK

Properly caring for any animal requires an understanding of the species and its place in the natural world. This includes digesting subjects as disparate as anatomy and ecology, diet and geography, and reproduction and physiology.

It is only by learning what your pet is, how it lives, what it does that you can achieve the primary goal of animal husbandry: Providing your pet with the highest quality of life possible.

Chapter 1: Blue-Tongued Skink Description and Anatomy

Like most other reptiles, blue-tongued skinks (*Tiliqua* spp.) have evolved a number of morphological adaptations to help them survive.

But although they certainly exhibit a few anatomical peculiarities, their body plan essentially resembles that of most other lizards.

Size

Blue-tongued skinks are medium to large lizards. Most adults reach lengths of between 14 and 24 inches (35 to 60 centimeters) in total length, with the tail representing up to half of this length (the relative tail size varies from one species and subspecies to the next). At maturity, most blue-tongued skinks weigh about 10 to 18 ounces (280 to 500 grams).

Young blue-tongued skinks are born measuring between 3 and 6 inches (7 to 15 centimeters) in length and weigh about 1/3- to 2/3-ounce (10 to 20 grams).

Scalation

Blue-tongued skinks are clad in very interesting-looking scales that are responsible to a large degree for their unique look.

You'll immediately notice that most of the scales overlap slightly and that they have a beaded appearance. Most of the scales are relatively uniform in size, although those on the flanks are slightly smaller than the rest, a few of the ones on the head are large and plate-like, and some of the ventral scales are large too. The scales on the legs are also somewhat small, and they become quite delicate-looking near the toes.

Interestingly, the scales of blue-tongued skinks contain small bony plates, called osteoderms. These provide additional rigidity to the scales and presumably provides a bit of extra protection from predators.

Color and Pattern

Each blue-tongued skink species possesses a characteristic color pattern, but there is great variation among individuals – even those hailing from the same litter.

The most commonly kept species – eastern blue-tongued skinks (*Tiliqua scincoides*) and Indonesian blue-tongued skinks (*Tiliqua gigas*) – are somewhat similar looking. They are both covered in dark brown ground colors and exhibit a row of bands or chevrons that travel down the back.

Centralian blue-tongued skinks (*Tiliqua multifasciata*) also exhibit a banded or striped pattern, although the colors present are usually much lighter than they are in the eastern and Indonesian species. The Western blue-tongued skink (*Tiliqua occipitalis*) is also banded, although the number of bands is greatly reduced.

The blotched blue-tongued skink (*Tiliqua nigrolutea*) has, as its name implies, a blotched pattern, consisting of a slightly chaotic set of bands, blotches and spots.

The shingleback skink (*Tiliqua rugosa*) varies from one subspecies to the next. Some are essentially patternless, others are banded and some have spots. The Adelaide pygmy skink (*Tiliqua adelaidensis*) is not kept in captivity, but it has a pale ground color, that is covered with speckles and spots of various sizes.

In most cases, the legs are covered in bands and other markings, while the tail pattern is a continuation of the dorsal pattern. The belly is usually white or lightly patterned.

Body, Head and Tail

While blue-tongued skinks have the same general body plan that other lizards do, meaning that they have four legs, a long body and a tail that is about half their body length, they aren't built like most other skinks.

Most skinks are long, leggy and lithe, but blue-tongued skinks are fairly short and squat, and their legs are quite short. Their tails are roughly similar in length to many other skinks, but they're far thicker than most.

Blue-tongued skinks also have large, triangular heads, and big eyes, which help them to spot predators and prey. Their tympanic membranes are visible and located at the rear of the head. The nostrils are located near the end of the snout, while their namesake blue tongues are held within the mouth.

Blue-tongued skinks have four short but muscular legs and each foot bears five long toes.

Vent

Like all other lizards, blue-tongued skinks possess a vent at the base of their tail. Located on the ventral side of the body, the vent serves as the exit point for urates and feces. It is also the place from which the hemipenes of males and the offspring produced by females emerge.

Internal Organs

The internal anatomy of blue-tongued skinks differs relatively little from that of other lizards.

Blue-tongued skinks draw oxygen in through their nostrils; pipe it through the trachea and into the lungs. Here, blood exchanges carbon dioxide for oxygen, before it is pumped to the various body parts via the heart and blood vessels.

While the hearts of blue-tongued skinks feature only three true chambers (two atria and a single ventricle), a septum keeps the ventricle divided at most times, allowing the heart to operate similarly to a four-chambered, mammalian heart.

This means that in practice, blue-tongued skinks keep their oxygenated and deoxygenated blood relatively separate in the heart.

Their digestive system is comprised of an esophagus, stomach, small intestine, large intestine and a terminal chamber called the cloaca. The stomach has some ability to stretch and accommodate food.

The liver resides near the center of the animal's torso, with the gallbladder sitting directly behind it. While the gallbladder stores bile, the liver provides a number of functions relating to digestion, metabolism and filtration.

Kidneys, which lie almost directly behind the lungs, filter wastes from the bloodstream.

Like other lizards, blue-tongued skinks control their bodies via their brain and nervous system. Their endocrine and exocrine glands work much as they do in other vertebrates.

Reproductive Organs
Like all squamates, blue-tongued skinks have paired reproductive organs, called hemipenes. When not in use, males keep their hemipenes inside the bases of their tails. When they attempt to mate with a female, they evert one of the hemipenes and insert it into the female's cloaca.

The paired nature of the male sex organs ensures that males can continue to breed if they suffer an injury to one of the hemipenes. This paired arrangement also allows male blue-tongued skinks to mate with females on either side of their body.

Unlike most other skinks, which are oviparous, and reproduce by laying shelled eggs, blue-tongued skinks are considered ovoviviparous, and they give live birth. Females have paired ovaries, which produce ova (eggs), and they have paired oviducts, which store the eggs after they are released from the ovaries. Once fertilized, the embryos develop inside individual amniotic sacs.

Birth occurs about three months later, and litters usually contain between 2 and 20 neonates.

Chapter 2: Blue-Tongued Skink Biology and Behavior

Blue-tongued skinks exhibit a number of biological and behavioral adaptations that allow them to survive in their natural habitats.

Shedding

Like other scaled reptiles, blue-tongued skinks shed their old skin to reveal new, fresh skin underneath.

Shedding may occur as often as every two to four weeks or as infrequently as twice a year. The rate at which a lizard sheds largely depends on its growth rate, although stress, illness and injury may also trigger rapid shed cycles.

Unlike snakes, which tend to shed in one long piece, blue-tongued skinks typically shed in several small pieces. Most blue-tongued skinks appear bolder and brighter immediately following a shed.

Metabolism and Digestion

Blue-tongued skinks are ectothermic ("cold-blooded") animals, whose internal metabolism depends on their body temperature. When warm, their bodily functions proceed more rapidly; when cold, their bodily functions proceed slowly.

This also means that the lizards digest more effectively at suitably warm temperatures than they do at suboptimal temperatures. Their appetites also vary with temperature, and if the temperatures drop below the preferred range, they may cease feeding entirely.

A blue-tongued skink's body temperature largely follows ambient air temperatures. They try to keep their body temperature within the preferred range by moving through the habitat while exploiting microhabitats of varying temperatures.

Typically, blue-tongued skinks emerge from their nocturnal hiding places and bask for one to four hours each morning. If necessary, they may bask again later in the day.

Growth Rate and Lifespan

Blue-tongued skinks have a moderate growth rate by lizard standards. Although the rate of growth varies according to a litany of factors – including species, sex, food availability and health – most take about 3 years to reach maturity.

Blue-tongued skinks also live for a fairly long time. However, as with most other small to medium-sized lizards, most blue-tongued skinks probably perish at the hands of predators before reaching their first birthday.

Nevertheless, most individuals who reach adulthood probably live for 5 years or more, and many probably survive for 10 or 15. Several captives have lived for longer than 10 years, and a few have reportedly reached the 20-year mark.

Foraging Behavior

Blue-tongued skinks actively forage for prey, but they only do so within a relatively small area. They typically prowl through the leaf litter, where they seek out edible vegetation, fruits, snails, worms, beetles and small vertebrates.

Different blue-tongued skink species exhibit slight differences in their foraging behavior, and individuals will even adjust their tactics to capitalize on the most common prey in the area.

Blue-tongued skinks are capable of climbing, but they rarely do so. Blue-tongued skinks can also swim, and some individuals commonly enter the water to soak or forage.

Diel and Seasonal Activity

Blue-tongued skinks are diurnal animals, who are most active in the early morning. They rarely move around or forage during the night.

Blue-tongued skinks exhibit different seasonal patterns depending on where they live. Some remain active all year long, while others may become dormant during exceptionally low winter temperatures.

Defensive Strategies and Tactics

Remaining out-of-sight is the first method by which blue-tongued skinks seek to defend themselves. They spend much of their time under or near some type of cover, such as leaf litter, rock piles or hollow logs.

If caught in the open, they typically rely on crypsis for protection. Their earth-tone colors help to break up their body shape, and they allow the lizards to blend in quite well in their natural habitats.

However, if the predator continues to approach, blue-tongued skinks may employ a unique defense strategy: They'll open their mouth widely and extend their bright blue tongue. This often startles predators, causing them to look elsewhere for an easier meal. If this fails to work, the lizards may also bite perceived threats or void the contents of their cloaca.

Reproduction

Blue-tongued skinks breed in the late spring or early summer, generally between September and December. However, the various species, subspecies and populations exhibit subtle differences in timing. Males often battle with other males over territory or breeding rights, although females rarely do.

The young are born about 100 days later, although the precise duration of the gestation period can vary slightly. The young may live near their parents for an extended period of time, although it doesn't appear as though any care is provided.

Chapter 3: Classification and Taxonomy

Like all other living species, blue-tongued skinks are placed within a hierarchical classification scheme. The highest levels of this classification scheme help distinguish groups like vertebrates from others, while the lower levels of classification distinguish blue-tongued skinks from other lizards.

As currently construed, the blue-tongued skink's classification scheme is as follows:

Kingdom: Animalia

Phylum: Chordata

Class: Reptilia

Order: Squamata

Family: Scincidae

Genus: *Tiliqua*

There are several species of blue-tongued skink, including:

- Adelaide pygmy blue-tongued skink (*Tiliqua adelaidensis*)

- Blotched blue-tongued skink (*Tiliqua nigrolutea*)

- Common blue-tongued skink (*Tiliqua scincoides*)

- Centralian blue-tongued skink (*Tiliqua multifasciata*)

- Indonesian blue-tongued skink (*Tiliqua gigas*)

- Shingleback blue-tongued skink (*Tiliqua rugosa*)

- Western blue-tongued skink (*Tiliqua occipitalis*)

Chapter 4: The Blue-Tongued Skink's World

As a group, blue-tongued skinks live across a pretty vast range that includes a variety of different habitats. And while these skinks are pretty flexible lizards, who are able to adjust to many different environmental conditions, most species and subspecies have evolved adaptations that allow them to live in the specific habitat type they call home.

The genus *Tiliqua* is found across most of Australia and New Guinea. There range includes a number of offshore islands too, including Tasmania and several islands between Australia and New Guinea.

They aren't found in the mountainous interior of New Guinea, but they do inhabit most of the Australian continent.

Individual species ranges and the characteristic habitats the lizards inhabit are listed below:

Adelaide Pygmy Blue-Tongue Skink
The pygmy blue-tongued skink has a very restricted range (they were thought extinct until rediscovered in 1992), that is limited to a very small area near Adelaide in South Australia.

Adelaide pygmy blue-tongued skinks are primarily found in grasslands, where they inhabit spider burrows.

Blotched Blue-Tongued Skink
Blotched blue-tongue skinks inhabit the southeastern corner of Australia, including parts of the Australian Capital Territory, New South Wales, Victoria, Tasmania and South Australia.

Blotched blue-tongued skinks primarily live in open habitats with plenty of ground cover, but they are also found in suburban areas.

Common Blue-Tongued Skink
The common blue-tongued skink has a large range that stretches from the northern coast of Western Australia, through the northern portion of the Northern Territory, and most of Queensland, New South Wales and the Australian Capital Territory. Their range extends across the southern portions of Australia, reaching into South Australia.

Common blue-tongued skinks live in a variety of different habitats across their range, including forests, grasslands, near-deserts and suburban areas. They do not, however, inhabit mountainous regions or rainforests.

Centralian Blue-Tongued Skink
As their name implies, Centralian blue-tongued skinks range across most of the Australian interior, including parts of Queensland and South Australia, as well as most of the Northern Territory and a significant portion of Western Australia.

Most Centralian blue-tongued skinks inhabit arid grasslands and deserts.

Indonesian Blue-Tongued Skink
The Indonesian blue-tongued skink is found around the periphery of the island of New Guinea. They are primarily restricted to the lowland rainforest areas along the coast, and they're absent from the interior mountains.

Shingleback Blue-Tongued Skink
The shingleback blue-tongued skink lives throughout most of the southern portions of Australia, including parts of Western

Australia, South Australia, New South Wales, The Australian Capital Territory, and Queensland.

Most shingleback blue-tongued skinks live in semi-arid grasslands, open forests and similar habitats.

Western Blue-Tongued Skink
As their name suggests, western blue-tongued skinks are found throughout the southern half of Western Australia, most of South Australia and small portions of the Northern Territory and New South Wales.

Western blue-tongued skinks inhabit a variety of different habitats, including grasslands, open forests and arid, desert-like regions.

Predators and Prey: The Blue-Tongued Skink's Food Web
The animals living alongside blue-tongued skinks play a big role in their lives. Some serve as food, while others represent potential predators.

Prey
A few of the most important food sources for blue-tongued skinks include:

- Insects (including beetles, caterpillars, grasshoppers, crickets, various larvae and others)

- Arachnids (including spiders and scorpions)

- Slugs and snails

- Small lizards

- Small snakes

- Rodents

- Frogs

- Potentially eggs (rarely)

Predators

Blue-tongued skinks have a number of biological and behavioral adaptations that help them defend themselves from predators. Nevertheless, they are regularly consumed by a few medium to large predators.

Some of the most important predators of blue-tongued skinks include:

- Predatory birds

- Large snakes

- Monitor lizards (goannas)

- Dingoes

- Domestic dogs and cats

PART II: BLUE-TONGUED SKINK HUSBANDRY

Once equipped with a basic understanding of what blue-tongued skinks *are* (Chapter 1 and Chapter 3), where they *live* (Chapter 4), and what they *do* (Chapter 2) you can begin learning about their captive care.

Animal husbandry is an evolving pursuit. Keepers shift their strategies frequently as they incorporate new information and ideas into their husbandry paradigms.

There are few "right" or "wrong" answers, and what works in one situation may not work in another. Accordingly, you may find that different authorities present different, and sometimes conflicting, information regarding the care of these lizards.

In all cases, you must strive to learn as much as you can about your pet and its natural habitat, so that you may provide it with the best quality of life possible.

Chapter 5: Blue-Tongued Skinks as Pets

Blue-tongued skinks can make rewarding pets, but you learn all you can about them before adding one to your home. This includes not only understanding the nature of the care they require but also the costs associated with this care.

Assuming that you feel confident in your ability to care for a blue-tongued skink and endure the associated financial burdens, you can begin seeking your individual pet.

Understanding the Commitment

Keeping a blue-tongued skink as a pet requires a substantial commitment. You will be responsible for your pet's well-being for the rest of its life. Blue-tongued skinks often live for 15 years or more, and you must be prepared to care for your new pet for this entire time.

Can you be sure that you will still want to care for your pet several years in the future? Do you know what your living situation will be? What changes will have occurred in your family? How will your working life have changed over this time?

You must consider all of these possibilities before acquiring a new pet. Failing to do so often leads to apathy, neglect and even resentment, which is not good for you or your pet blue-tongued skink.

Neglecting your pet is wrong, and in some locations, a criminal offense. You must continue to provide quality care for your blue-tongued skink, even once the novelty has worn off, and it is no longer fun to clean the cage and provide him with insects each week.

Once you purchase a blue-tongued skink, its well-being becomes your responsibility until it passes away at the end of a long life, or you have found someone who will agree to adopt the animal for you. Unfortunately, this is rarely an easy task. You may begin with thoughts of selling your pet to help recoup a small part of your investment, but these efforts will largely fall flat.

While professional breeders may profit from the sale of blue-tongued skinks, amateurs are at a decided disadvantage. Only a tiny sliver of the general population is interested in reptilian pets, and only a small subset of these are interested in keeping blue-tongued skinks.

Of those who are interested in acquiring a blue-tongued skink, most would rather start fresh, by *purchasing* a small hatchling or juvenile from an established breeder, rather than adopting your questionable animal *for free.*

After having difficulty finding a willing party to purchase or adopt your animal, many owners try to donate their pet to a local zoo. Unfortunately, this rarely works either.

Zoos are not interested in your blue-tongued skink, no matter how pretty he is. He is a pet with little to no reliable provenance and questionable health status. This is simply not the type of animal zoos are eager to add to their multi-million-dollar collections.

Zoos obtain most of their animals from other zoos and museums; failing that, they obtain their animals directly from their land of origin. As a rule, they do not accept donated pets.

No matter how difficult it becomes to find a new home for your unwanted blue-tongued skink, you must never release non-native reptiles into the wild.

The Costs of Captivity

Reptiles are often marketed as low-cost pets. While true in a relative sense (the costs associated with dog, cat, horse or tropical fish husbandry are often much higher than they are for blue-tongued skinks), potential keepers must still prepare for the financial implications of reptile ownership.

At the outset, you must budget for the acquisition of your pet, as well as the costs of purchasing or constructing a habitat. Unfortunately, while many keepers plan for these costs, they typically fail to consider the on-going costs, which will quickly eclipse the initial startup costs.

Startup Costs

One surprising fact most new keepers learn is the enclosure and equipment will often cost as much as (or more than) the animal does (except in the case of very high-priced specimens).

Prices fluctuate from one market to the next, but in general, the least you will spend on a healthy blue-tongued skink is about $100 (£70); you'll also need to spend another $50 (£36) on his initial habitat and care equipment. Replacement equipment and food will represent additional (and ongoing) expenses.

Ongoing Costs

The ongoing costs of blue-tongued skink ownership primarily fall into one of three categories: food, maintenance and veterinary care.

Food costs are the most significant of the three, but they are relatively consistent and somewhat predictable. Some maintenance costs are easy to calculate, but things like equipment malfunctions are impossible to predict with any certainty. Veterinary expenses are hard to predict and vary wildly from one year to the next.

Food Costs

Food is the single greatest ongoing cost you will experience while caring for your blue-tongued skink. To obtain a reasonable estimate of your yearly food costs, you must consider the number of meals you will feed your pet per year and the cost of each meal.

The amount of food your blue-tongued skink will consume will vary based on numerous factors, including his size, the average temperatures in his habitat and his health.

As a ballpark number, you should figure that you'll need about $2 (£1.50) per week – roughly $100 (£70) per year -- for food. You could certainly spend more or less than this, but that is a reasonable estimate for back-of-the-envelope calculations.

Veterinary Costs

While you should always seek veterinary advice at the first sign of illness, it is probably not wise to haul your healthy blue-tongued skink to the vet's office for no reason – they don't require "checkups" or annual vaccinations as some other pets may. Accordingly, you shouldn't incur any veterinary expenses unless your pet falls ill.

However, veterinary care can become very expensive, very quickly. In addition to a basic exam or phone consultation, your blue-tongued skink may need cultures, x-rays or other diagnostic tests performed. In light of this, wise keepers budget at least $200 to $300 (£160 to £245) each year to cover any emergency veterinary costs.

Maintenance Costs

It is important to plan for both routine and unexpected maintenance costs. Commonly used items, such as paper towels, disinfectant and topsoil are rather easy to calculate. However, it is not easy to know how many burned out light bulbs, cracked misting units or faulty thermostats you will have to replace in a given year.

Those who keep their blue-tongued skinks in simple enclosures will find that about $50 (£40) covers their yearly maintenance costs. By contrast, those who maintain elaborate habitats may spend $200 (£160) or more each year.

Always try to purchase frequently used supplies, such as light bulbs, paper towels and disinfectants in bulk to maximize your savings. It is often beneficial to consult with local reptile-keeping clubs, who often pool their resources to attain greater buying power.

Myths and Misunderstandings

Unfortunately, there are many myths and misunderstandings about blue-tongued skink and reptile-keeping in general. Some myths represent outdated thinking or techniques, while other myths and misunderstandings reflect the desires of keepers, rather than the reality of the situation.

Myth: *Blue-tongued skinks are reptiles, so they are not capable of suffering or feeling pain.*

Fact: While it is important to avoid anthropomorphizing or projecting human emotions and motivations to non-human entities, reptiles – including blue-tongued skinks – feel pain. There is no doubt that they can experience pain and seek to avoid it. While it is impossible to know exactly what a blue-tongued skink thinks, there is no reason to believe that they do not suffer similarly to other animals, when injured, ill or depressed.

Myth: *My blue-tongued skink likes to be held so he can feel the warmth of my hands.*

Fact: Generally speaking, blue-tongued skinks do not like to be handled or held, although they may tolerate more keeper interaction than many other lizards will. The myth that reptiles enjoy the heat from a person's hands springs from the notion that because reptiles are "cold-blooded," and they must derive their heat from external sources, they must enjoy warmth at all times. However, this is an oversimplification of their behavior.

Myth: *Blue-tongued skinks are good pets for young children.*

Fact: While many reptiles, including blue-tongued skinks, make wonderful pets for adults, teenagers and families, they require more care than a young child can provide. The age at which a child is capable of caring for a pet will vary, but children should be about 10 to 12 years of age before they are allowed to care for their own blue-tongued skink. Parents must exercise prudent judgment and make a sound assessment of their child's capabilities and maturity. Children will certainly enjoy pet reptiles, but they must be cared for by someone with adequate maturity. Additionally, it is important to consider the potential for young children contracting salmonella and other pathogens from the family pet.

Myth: *If you get tired of a blue-tongued skink, it is easy to find a new home for it. The zoo will surely want your pet; after all, you are giving it to them free of charge! If that doesn't work, you can always just release it into the wild.*

Fact: Acquiring a pet blue-tongued skink is a very big commitment. If you ever decide that your pet no longer fits your family or lifestyle, you may have a tough time finding a suitable home for it. You can attempt to sell the animal, but this is illegal in some places, and often requires a permit or license to do legally.

Zoos and pet stores will be reticent to accept your pet – even at no charge – because they cannot be sure that your pet does not have an illness that could spread through their collections. A zoo may have to spend hundreds or thousands of dollars for the care, housing and veterinary care to accept your pet blue-tongued skink, and such things are not taken lightly.

Some people consider releasing their blue-tongued skink into the wild if no other accommodations can be made, but such acts are destructive, often illegal and usually a death sentence for the lizard.

Acquiring Your Blue-Tongued Skink

Modern reptile enthusiasts can acquire blue-tongued skinks from a variety of sources, each with a different set of pros and cons.

Pet stores are one of the first places many people see blue-tongued skinks, and they become the de facto source of pets for many beginning keepers. While they do offer some unique benefits to prospective keepers, pet stores are not always the best place to purchase a pet reptile; so, consider all of the available options, including breeders and reptile swap meets, before making a purchase.

Pet Stores

Pet stores offer a number of benefits to keepers shopping for blue-tongued skinks, including convenience: They usually stock all of the equipment your new lizard needs, including cages, heating devices and food items.

Additionally, they offer you the chance to inspect the blue-tongued skinks up close before purchase. In some cases, you may be able to choose from more than one specimen. Many pet stores provide health guarantees for a short period, which provide some recourse if your new pet turns out to be ill.

However, pet stores are not always the ideal place to purchase your new pet. Pet stores are retail establishments, and as such, you will usually pay more for your new pet than you would from a breeder.

Additionally, pet stores rarely know the pedigree of the animals they sell, and they will rarely know the blue-tongued skink's date of birth or other pertinent information.

Other drawbacks associated with pet stores primarily relate to the staff's inexperience. While some pet stores concentrate on reptiles and may educate their staff about proper blue-tongued skink care, many others provide incorrect advice to their customers.

It is also worth considering the increased exposure to pathogens that pet store animals endure, given the constant flow of animals through such facilities.

Reptile Expos

Reptile expos offer another option for purchasing blue-tongued skinks. Reptile expos often feature resellers, breeders and retailers in the same room, all selling various types of blue-tongued skinks and other reptiles.

Often, the prices at such events are quite reasonable and you are often able to select from many different blue-tongued skinks. However, if you have a problem, it may be difficult to find the seller after the event is over.

Breeders

Because they usually offer unparalleled information and support to their customers, breeders are generally the best place for most novices to shop for blue-tongued skinks. Additionally, breeders often know the species well and are better able to help you learn the husbandry techniques necessary for success.

The primary disadvantage of buying from a breeder is that you must often make such purchases from a distance, either by phone or via the internet. Nevertheless, most established breeders are happy to provide you with photographs of the animal you will be purchasing, as well as his or her parents.

Selecting Your Blue-Tongued Skink

Not all blue-tongued skinks are created equally, so it is important to select a healthy individual that will give you the best chance of success.

Practically speaking, the most important criterion to consider is the health of the animal. However, the sex, age and history of the blue-tongued skink are also important things to consider.

Health Checklist

Always check your blue-tongued skink thoroughly for signs of injury or illness before purchasing it. If you are purchasing the animal from someone in a different part of the country, you must inspect it immediately upon delivery. Notify the seller promptly if the animal exhibits any health problems.

Avoid the temptation to acquire or accept a sick or injured animal in hopes of nursing him back to health. Not only are you likely to incur substantial veterinary costs while treating your new pet, you will likely fail in your attempts to restore the blue-tongued skink to full health. Sick animals rarely recover in the hands of novices.

A blue-tongued skink with its tongue extended.

Additionally, by purchasing injured or diseased animals, you incentivize poor husbandry on the part of the retailer. If retailers lose money on sick or injured animals, they will take steps to avoid this eventuality, by acquiring healthier stock in the first place and providing better care for their charges.

As much as is possible, try to observe the following features:

- Observe the animal's skin. It should be free of lacerations and other damage. Pay special attention to those areas that frequently sustain damage, such as the tail and the front of the face. A small cut or abrasion may be relatively easy to treat, but significant abrasions and cuts are likely to become infected and require significant treatment.

- **Gently check the animal's crevices and creases for mites and ticks**. Avoid purchasing any animal that has ectoparasites. Additionally, you should avoid purchasing any other animals from this source, as they are likely to harbor parasites as well.

- **Examine the animal's eyes and nostrils**. The eyes should not be sunken, and they should be free of discharge. The nostrils should be clear and dry – skinks with runny noses or those who blow bubbles are likely to be suffering from a respiratory infection.

- **Gently palpate the animal and ensure no lumps or anomalies are apparent**. Lumps in the muscles or abdominal cavity may indicate parasites, abscesses or tumors.

- **Observe the animal's demeanor**. Healthy blue-tongued skinks are aware of their environment and react to stimuli. When active, the animal should calmly explore his environment. Avoid lethargic animals, which do not appear alert.

- **Check the animal's vent**. The vent should be clean and free of smeared feces. Smeared feces can indicate parasites or bacterial infections.

The Age

Hatchling blue-tongued skinks are very fragile until they reach about three or four months of age. Before this, they are unlikely to thrive in the hands of beginning keepers.

Accordingly, most beginners should purchase four- or five-month-old juveniles, who have already become well established. Animals of this age tolerate the changes associated with a new home better than very young specimens do. Further, given their larger size, they will better tolerate temperature and humidity extremes than smaller animals will.

The Sex

Unless you are attempting to breed blue-tongued skinks, you should select a male pet, as females are more likely to suffer from reproduction-related health problems than males are.

But those simply seeking a pet can easily avoid this unnecessary complication by selecting a male.

Quarantine

Because new animals may have illnesses or parasites that could infect the rest of your collection, it is wise to quarantine all new acquisitions. This means that you should keep any new animal as separated from the rest of your pets as possible. Only once you have ensured that the new animal is healthy should you introduce it to the rest of your collection.

During the quarantine period, you should keep the new blue-tongued skink in a simplified habitat, with a paper substrate, water bowl, several branches, basking spot and a few hiding places. Keep the temperature and humidity at ideal levels.

It is wise to obtain fecal samples from your blue-tongued skink during the quarantine period. You can take these samples to your veterinarian, who can check them for signs of internal parasites. Always treat any existing parasite infestations before removing the animal from quarantine.

Always tend to quarantined animals last, as this reduces the chances of transmitting pathogens to your healthy animals. Do not wash quarantined water bowls or cage furniture with those belonging to your healthy animals. Whenever possible, use completely separate tools for quarantined animals and those that have been in your collection for some time.

Always be sure to wash your hands thoroughly after handling quarantined animals, their cages or their tools. Particularly careful keepers wear a smock or alternative clothing when handling quarantined animals.

Quarantine new acquisitions for a minimum of 30 days; 60 or 90 days is even better. Many zoos and professional breeders maintain 180- or 360-day-long quarantine periods.

Chapter 6: Providing the Captive Habitat

Providing your blue-tongued skink with appropriate housing is an essential aspect of captive care. In essence, the habitat you provide to your pet becomes his "world."

In "the old days," those inclined to keep reptiles had few choices with regard to caging. The two primary options were to build a custom cage from scratch or construct a lid to use with a fish aquarium.

By contrast, modern hobbyists have a variety of options from which to choose. In addition to building custom cages or adapting aquaria, dozens of different cage styles are available – each with different pros and cons.

Dimensions

Throughout their lives, reptiles need a cage large enough to lay comfortably, access a range of temperatures and get enough room for exercise. In the case of blue-tongued skinks, 6 to 8 square feet is usually sufficient.

But understand that this represents the *minimum* amount of space your pets require. Always strive to offer the largest cage that you reasonably can. While many keepers suggest that large cages are intimidating to lizards and other reptiles, the truth is subtler. Contrary to the popular notion, large cages – in and of themselves – do not cause reptiles to experience stress.

Blue-tongued skinks live in habitats that exceed even the largest cages by several orders of magnitude. What they do not do, however, is spend much time exposed.

Large, barren cages that do not feature complex cage props and numerous hiding places may very well stress them. However, large, *complex* habitats afford more space for exercising and exploring in addition to allowing for the establishment of a superb thermal gradient.

In addition to total space, the layout of the cage is also important – rectangular cages are strongly preferred for a variety of reasons:

- They allow the keeper to establish more drastic heat gradients.

- Enclosures with one long direction allow your animals to stretch out and crawl around more than square cage do.

- Front opening cages are easier to maintain when the cages are rectangular, as you do not have to reach as far back into the cage to reach the back wall.

Aquariums

Aquariums are popular choices for skink cages, largely because of their ubiquity. Virtually any pet store that carries blue-tongued skinks will also stock aquariums.

Aquariums can make suitable blue-tongued skink cages, but they have a number of drawbacks. For starters, glass cages are hard to clean, and they are easy to break while you are carrying them around. Additionally, large aquariums are usually extremely heavy.

Aquariums are only enclosed on five sides, so keepers have to purchase or build a suitable lid for the enclosure. After-market screen tops are available, but often, they are not secure enough for escape-prone reptiles. Fortunately, blue-tongued skinks are not terribly skilled escape artists.

Commercial Cages

Commercially produced cages have a number of benefits over other enclosures. Commercial cages usually feature doors on the front of the cage, allowing them to provide better access than top-opening cages do. Additionally, bypass glass doors or framed, hinged doors are generally more secure than after-market screened lids (as are used on aquariums) are.

Additionally, plastic cages are usually produced in dimensions that make more sense for reptiles and often have features that aid in heating and lighting the cage.

Commercial cages can be made out of wood, metal, glass or other substances, but the majority are PVC or ABS plastic.

Commercially cages are available in two primary varieties: those that are molded from one piece of plastic and those that are assembled from several different sheets. Assembled cages are less expensive and easier to construct, but molded cages have few (if any) seams or cracks in which bacteria and other pathogens can hide.

Some cage manufacturers produce cages in multiple colors. White is probably the best color for novices, as it is easy to see dirt, mites and other small problems. A single mite crawling on a white cage surface is very visible, even from a distance.

Black cages do not show dirt as well. This can be helpful for more experienced keepers who have developed proper hygiene techniques over time. Additionally, blue-tongued skinks often look very sharp against black cage walls.

While blue-tongued skinks can probably see colors, it is unlikely that cage color is a significant factor in their quality of life. If you worry about the selection of color, it is probably best to choose a dark or earth-toned color.

Plastic Storage Containers

Plastic storage containers, such as those used for shoes, sweaters or food, make suitable cages for blue-tongued skinks if they are customized to meet your lizards' needs. However, as with aquaria, the lids for plastic storage boxes are rarely secure enough to be used for reptile maintenance without the addition of supplemental security measures.

Hobbyists and breeders overcome this by incorporating Velcro straps, hardware latches or other strategies into plastic storage container cages. While these can be secure, you must be sure they are 100 percent escape-proof before placing your pet in such cages.

The safest way to use plastic storage containers is with the use of a wooden or plastic rack. In such systems, often called "lidless" systems, the shelves of the rack form the top to the cage sitting below them. The gap between the top of the sides of the storage containers and the bottom of the shelves is usually very tight – approximately one-eighth inch or less.

When plastic containers are used, you must drill or melt numerous holes for air exchange. If you are using a lid, it is acceptable to place the holes in the lid; however, if you are using a lidless system, you will have to make the holes in the sides of the boxes.

All holes should be made from the inside towards the outside. This will help reduce the chances of leaving sharp edges inside the cage, which could cut your pets.

Homemade Cages

For keepers with access to tools and the desire and skill to use them, it is possible to construct homemade cages. However, this is not recommended for novice keepers, who do not yet have experience keeping reptiles.

A number of materials are suitable for cage construction, and each has different pros and cons. Wood is commonly used but must be adequately sealed to avoid rotting, warping or absorbing offensive odors.

Plastic sheeting is a very good material, but few have the necessary skills, knowledge and tools necessary for cage construction. Additionally, some plastics may have extended off-gassing times.

Glass can be used, whether glued to itself or with used with a frame. Custom-built glass cages can be better than aquariums, as you can design them in dimensions that are appropriate for blue-tongued skinks. Additionally, they can be constructed in such a way that the door is on the front of the cage, rather than the top.

Screen Cages

Screen cages make excellent habitats for some lizards and frogs, but they are poorly suited for most blue-tongued skinks – particularly those species and subspecies that hail from humid habitats.

Screened cages simply won't maintain a high enough humidity level to keep your lizards healthy, even if you mist the enclosure constantly.

Screened enclosures can be used for species and subspecies native to arid regions, but they still present several challenges when used in this way. For starters, screened enclosures are difficult to heat efficiently. You'll often need to use more heating devices to achieve proper temperatures for your lizard.

Additionally, screen cages are difficult to clean, as dirt and debris can become wedged between the screen strands. Additionally, your blue-tongued skink's claws may cause weak spots to develop. In a worst-case scenario, such weak spots can allow blue-tongued skinks to push through and escape.

Chapter 7: Heating the Habitat

Providing the proper thermal environment is one of the most important aspects of reptile husbandry. As ectothermic ("cold-blooded") animals, blue-tongued skinks rely on the surrounding temperatures to regulate the rate at which their metabolism operates.

Providing a proper thermal environment can mean the difference between a healthy, thriving pet and one who spends a great deal of time at the veterinarian's office, battling infections and illness.

While individuals may demonstrate slightly different preferences and different species have slightly different preferences, blue-tongued skinks prefer ambient temperatures in the mid-80s Fahrenheit (between 28 and 31 degrees Celsius). Inactive (sleeping) blue-tongued skinks prefer temperatures in the mid-70s Fahrenheit (22 to 23 degrees Celsius).

Blue-tongued skinks don't appear to bask very much, but many hobbyists find it helpful to provide a slightly warmer basking spot in the habitat. The basking spot's temperature should be around 90 degrees Fahrenheit (32 degrees Celsius).

Providing your blue-tongued skink with a suitable thermal environment requires the correct approach, the correct heating equipment and the tools necessary for monitoring the thermal environment.

Size-Related Heating Concerns

Before examining the best way to establish a proper thermal environment, it is important to understand that your lizard's body size influences the way in which he heats up and cools off.

Because volume increases more quickly than surface area does with increasing body size, small individuals experience more rapid temperature fluctuations than larger individuals do.

Accordingly, it is imperative to protect small individuals from temperature extremes. Conversely, larger blue-tongued skinks are more tolerant of temperature extremes than smaller individuals are (though they should still be protected from temperature extremes).

Thermal Gradients

In the wild, blue-tongued skinks move between different microhabitats so that they can maintain ideal body temperature as much as possible.

The best way to do this is by clustering the heating devices at one end of the habitat, thereby creating a basking spot (the warmest spot in the enclosure).

The temperatures will slowly drop with increasing distance from the basking spot, which creates a *gradient* of temperatures. Barriers, such as branches and vegetation, also help to create shaded patches, which provide additional thermal options.

This mimics the way temperatures vary from one small place to the next in your pet's natural habitat. By establishing a gradient in the enclosure, your captive blue-tongued skink will be able to access a range of different temperatures, which will allow him to manage his body temperature just as his wild counterparts do.

Adjust the heating device until the surface temperatures at the basking spot are about 90 degrees Fahrenheit (32 degrees Celsius). Provide a slightly cooler basking spot for immature individuals.

Because there is no heat source at the other end of the cage, the ambient temperature will gradually fall as your lizard moves away from the heat source. Ideally, the cool end of the cage should be in the low 70s Fahrenheit (22 degrees Celsius).

The need to establish a thermal gradient is one of the most compelling reasons to use a roomy cage. In general, the larger the cage, the easier it is to establish a suitable thermal gradient.

Heating Equipment

There are a variety of different heating devices you can use to keep your blue-tongued skink's habitat within the appropriate temperature range.

Be sure to consider your choice carefully and select the best type of heating device for you and your pet.

Heat Lamps

Heat lamps are usually the best choice for supplying heat to your pet's habitat. Heat lamps consist of a reflector dome and an incandescent bulb. The light bulb produces heat (in addition to light) and the metal reflector dome directs the heat to a spot inside the cage.

You will need to clamp the lamp to a stable anchor or part of the cage's frame. Always be sure that the lamp is securely attached and will not be dislodged by vibration, children or pets.

Because fire safety is always a concern, and many keepers use high-wattage light bulbs, opt for heavy-duty reflector domes with ceramic bases, rather than economy units with plastic bases. The price difference is negligble, given the stakes.

One of the greatest benefits of using heat lamps to maintain the temperature of your pet's habitat is the flexibility they offer. While you can adjust the amount of heat provided by heat tapes and other devices with a rheostat or thermostat, you can adjust the enclosure temperature provided by heat lamps in two ways:

- Changing the Bulb Wattage

The simplest way to adjust the temperature of your pet's cage is by changing the wattage of the bulb you are using.

For example, if a 40-watt light bulb is not raising the temperature of the basking spot high enough, you may try a 60-watt bulb. Alternatively, if a 100-watt light bulb is elevating the cage temperatures higher than are appropriate, switching to a 60-watt bulb may help.

- Adjusting the Distance between the Heat Lamp and the Basking Spot

The closer the heat lamp is to the cage, the warmer the cage will be. If the habitat is too warm, you can move the light farther from the enclosure, which should lower the basking spot temperatures slightly.

However, the farther away you move the lamp, the larger the basking spot becomes. It is important to be careful that you do not move it too far away, which will reduce the effectiveness of the thermal gradient by heating the enclosure too uniformly. In very large cages, this may not compromise the thermal gradient very much, but in a small cage, it may eliminate the "cool side" of the habitat.

In other words, if your heat lamp creates a basking spot that is roughly 1-foot in diameter when it is 1 inch away from the screen, it will produce a slightly cooler, but larger basking spot when moved back another 6 inches or so.

Ceramic Heat Emitters

Ceramic heat emitters are small inserts that function similarly to light bulbs, except that they do not produce any visible light – they only produce heat.

Ceramic heat emitters are used in reflector-dome fixtures, just as heat lamps are. The benefits of such devices are numerous:

- They typically last much longer than light bulbs do

- They are suitable for use with thermostats

- They allow for the creation of overhead basking spots, as lights do

- They can be used day or night

However, the devices do have three primary drawbacks:

- They are very hot when in operation

- They are much more expensive than light bulbs

- You cannot tell by looking if they are hot or cool. This can be a safety hazard – touching a ceramic heat emitter while it is hot is likely to cause serious burns.

Radiant Heat Panels

Quality radiant heat panels are a great choice for heating most reptile habitats, including those containing blue-tongued skinks. Radiant heat panels are essentially heat pads that stick to the roof of the habitat. They usually feature rugged, plastic or metal casings and internal reflectors to direct the infrared heat back into the cage.

Radiant heat panels have a number of benefits over traditional heat lamps and under tank heat pads:

- They do not produce visible light, which means they are useful for both diurnal and nocturnal heat production. They can be used in conjunction with fluorescent light fixtures during the day and remain on at night once the lights go off.

- They are inherently flexible. Unlike many devices that do not work well with pulse-proportional thermostats, most radiant heat panels work well with on-off and pulse-proportional thermostats.

The only real drawback to radiant heat panels is their cost: radiant heat panels often cost about two to three times the price of light- or heat pad-oriented systems. However, many radiant heat panels outlast light bulbs and heat pads, a fact that offsets their high initial cost over the long term.

Heat Pads
Heat pads are an attractive option for many new keepers, but they are not without drawbacks.

- Heat pads have a high risk of causing contact burns.

- If they malfunction, they can damage the cage as well as the surface on which they are placed.

- They are more likely to cause a fire than heat lamps or radiant heat panels are.

However, if installed properly (which includes allowing fresh air to flow over the exposed side of the heat pad) and used in conjunction with a thermostat, they can be reasonably safe. With heat pads, it behooves the keeper to purchase premium products, despite the small increase in price.

Heat Tape

Heat tape is somewhat akin to a "stripped down" heat pad. In fact, most heat pads are simply pieces of heat tape that have already been connected and sealed inside a plastic envelope.

Heat tape is primarily used to heat large numbers of cages simultaneously. It is generally inappropriate for novices and requires the keeper to make electrical connections. Additionally, a thermostat is always required when using heat tape.

Historically, heat tape was used to keep water pipes from freezing – not to heat reptile cages. While some commercial heat tapes have been designed specifically for reptiles, many have not. Accordingly, it may be illegal, not to mention dangerous, to use heat tapes for purposes other than for which they are designed.

Heat Cables

Heat cables are similar to heat tape, in that they heat a long strip of the cage, but they are much more flexible and easy to use. Many heat cables are suitable to use inside the cage, while others are designed for use outside the habitat.

Always be sure to purchase heat cables that are designed to be used in reptile cages. Those sold at hardware stores are not appropriate for use in a cage.

Heat cables must be used in conjunction with a thermostat, or, at the very least, a rheostat.

Nocturnal Temperatures

Because blue-tongued skinks easily tolerate temperatures in the low-70s Fahrenheit (21 to 22 degrees Celsius) at night, most keepers can allow their pet's habitat to fall to ambient room temperature at night.

Because it is important to avoid using lights on your lizard's habitat at night, those living in homes with lower nighttime temperatures will need to employ additional heat sources. Most such keepers accomplish this through the use of ceramic heat emitters.

Thermometers

It is important to monitor the cage temperatures very carefully to ensure your pet stays healthy. Just as a water test kit is an aquarist's best friend, quality thermometers are some of the most important husbandry tools for reptile keepers.

Ambient and Surface Temperatures

Two different types of temperature are relevant for pet blue-tongued skinks: ambient temperatures and surface temperatures.

The ambient temperature in your animal's enclosure is the air temperature; the surface temperatures are the temperatures of the objects in the cage. Both are important to monitor, as they can differ widely.

Measure the cage's ambient temperatures with a digital thermometer. An indoor-outdoor model will feature a probe that allows you to measure the temperature at both ends of the thermal gradient at once. For example, you may position the thermometer at the cool side of the cage but attach the remote probe to a branch near the basking spot.

Because standard digital thermometers do not measure surface temperatures well, use a non-contact, infrared thermometer for such measurements. These devices will allow you to measure surface temperatures accurately from a short distance away.

Thermostats and Rheostats

Some heating devices, such as heat lamps, are designed to operate at full capacity for the entire time that they are turned on.

Such devices should not be used with thermostats – instead, care should be taken to calibrate the proper temperature by tweaking the bulb wattage.

Other devices, such as heat pads, heat tape and radiant heat panels are designed to be used with a regulating device, such as a thermostat or rheostat, which maintains the proper temperature

Rheostats

Rheostats are similar to light-dimmer switches, and they allow you to reduce the output of a heating device. In this way, you can dial in the proper temperature for the habitat.

The drawback to rheostats is that they only regulate the amount of power going to the device – they do not monitor the cage temperature or adjust the power flow automatically. In practice, even with the same level of power entering the device, the amount of heat generated by most heat sources will vary over the course of the day.

If you set the rheostat so that it keeps the cage at the right temperature in the morning, it may become too hot by the middle of the day. Conversely, setting the proper temperature during the middle of the day may leave the morning temperatures too cool.

Care must be taken to ensure that the rheostat controller is not inadvertently bumped or jostled, causing the temperature to rise or fall outside of healthy parameters.

Thermostats

Thermostats are similar to rheostats, except that they also feature a temperature probe that monitors the temperature in the cage (or under the basking source). This allows the thermostat to adjust the power going to the device as necessary to maintain a predetermined temperature.

For example, if you place the temperature probe under a basking spot powered by a radiant heat panel, the thermostat will keep the temperature relatively constant at the basking site.

There are two different types of thermostats:

- On-Off Thermostats

On-Off Thermostats work by cutting the power to the device when the probe's temperature reaches a given temperature.

For example, if the thermostat were set to 85 degrees Fahrenheit (29 degrees Celsius), the heating device would turn off whenever the temperature exceeds this threshold. When the temperature falls below 85, the thermostat restores power to the unit, and the heater begins functioning again.

This cycle will continue to repeat, thus maintaining the temperature within a relatively small range.

Be aware that on-off thermostats have a "lag" factor, meaning that they do not turn off when the temperature reaches a given temperature. They turn off when the temperature is a few degrees above that temperature, and then turn back on when the temperate is a little below the set point.

Because of this, it is important to avoid setting the temperature at the limits of your pet's acceptable range. Some premium models have an adjustable amount of threshold for this factor, which is helpful.

- Pulse Proportional Thermostats

Pulse proportional thermostats work by constantly sending pulses of electricity to the heater. By varying the rate of pulses, the amount of energy reaching the heating devices varies. A small computer inside the thermostat adjusts this rate to match the set-point temperature as measured by the probe. Accordingly, pulse proportional thermostats maintain much more consistent temperatures than on-off thermostats do.

Lights should not be used with thermostats, as the constant flickering may stress your pet. Conversely, heat pads, heat tape, radiant heat panels and ceramic heat emitters should always be used with either a rheostat or, preferably, a thermostat to avoid overheating your pet.

Thermostat Failure

If used for long enough, all thermostats eventually fail. The question is will yours fail today or twenty years from now.

While some thermostats fail in the "off" position, a thermostat that fails in the "on" position may overheat your lizard. Unfortunately, tales of entire collections being lost to a faulty thermostat are too common.

Accordingly, it behooves the keeper to acquire high-quality thermostats. Some keepers use two thermostats, connected in a series arrangement.

By setting the second thermostat (the "backup thermostat") a few degrees higher than the setting used on the "primary thermostat," you safeguard yourself against the failure of either unit.

In such a scenario, the backup thermostat allows the full power coming to it to travel through to the heating device, as the temperature never reaches its higher set-point temperature.

However, if the first unit fails in the "on" position, the second thermostat will keep the temperatures from rising too high. The temperature will rise a few degrees in accordance with the higher set-point temperature, but it will not get hot enough to harm your pets.

If the backup thermostat fails in the "on" position, the first thermostat retains control. If either fails in the "off" position, the temperature will fall until you rectify the situation, but a brief exposure to relatively cool temperatures is unlikely to be fatal.

Chapter 8: Lighting the Enclosure

Lighting is a contentious and controversial subject among lizard keepers. This is especially true among blue-tongued skink keepers, as their lighting needs are not entirely clear. Accordingly, most keepers elect to err on the side of caution and provide their lizards with full-spectrum lighting, just as many other lizard keepers do for their captives.

However, it can be difficult to provide full-spectrum lighting indoors. Additionally, you'll want to ensure that your lizard is receiving the wavelengths of light he needs to remain healthy.

Accordingly, there is a great deal such keepers must understand about light to make sure they meet their pet's needs.

Light for Viewing

Even if you don't think that full-spectrum lighting is necessary for your lizard's health, you may want to use some form of lighting to help make your blue-tongued skink and his habitat easier to view.

If you use a heat lamp to provide a thermal gradient, the light from the bulb will provide more than enough illumination to appreciate your pet's habits and habitat.

But you can also add a fluorescent fixture to your pet's cage to illuminate it. An ordinary fluorescent bulb will suffice for this purpose, but you can also select a premium model, designed to produce more balanced light. This will make the colors in the cage more appealing, and it may help your plants to stay healthier.

You can also use a red-colored light at night, but this is only necessary if you need to provide supplemental heat when the primary basking lights are off. Blue-tongued skinks are rarely active at night, so you won't be missing anything if you allow his enclosure to become completely dark.

Light for Health

As stated earlier, most keepers provide full-spectrum lighting for their blue-tongued skinks. But before you can do so, you'll need to learn a little bit about light.

Light is a type of energy that physicists call electromagnetic radiation; it travels in waves. These waves may differ in amplitude, which correlates to the vertical distance between consecutive wave crests and troughs, frequency, which correlates with the number of crests per unit of time, and wavelength.

Wavelength is the distance from one crest to the next or one trough to the next. Wavelength and frequency are inversely proportional, meaning that as the wavelength increases, the frequency decreases. It is more common for reptile keepers to discuss wavelengths rather than frequencies.

The sun produces energy (light) with a very wide range of constituent wavelengths. Some of these wavelengths fall within a range called the visible spectrum; humans can detect these rays with their eyes. Such waves have wavelengths between about 390 and 700 nanometers. Rays with wavelengths longer or shorter than these limits are broken into their own groups and given different names.

Those rays with around 390-nanometer wavelengths or less are called ultraviolet rays or UV rays. UV rays are broken down into three different categories, just as the different colors correspond with different wavelengths of visible light.

UVA rays have wavelengths between 315 to 400 nanometers, while UVB rays have wavelengths between 280 and 315 nanometers while UVC rays have wavelengths between 100 and 280 nanometers.

Rays with wavelengths of less than 280 nanometers are called x-rays and gamma rays. At the other end of the spectrum, infrared rays have wavelengths longer than 700 nanometers; microwaves and radio waves are even longer.

UVA rays are important for food recognition, appetite, activity and eliciting natural behaviors in some species. UVB rays are necessary for many reptiles to produce vitamin D3. Without this vitamin, sun-dependent reptiles cannot properly metabolize their calcium.

Chapter 9: Enclosure Furniture

Strictly speaking, it is possible to keep a blue-tongued skink in a cage devoid of anything but a substrate that permits burrowing and a water bowl. However, it is wise to provide blue-tongued skinks with complex environments, containing several places to hide, burrow and explore.

Additionally, many keepers enjoy decorating the cage to resemble the animal's natural habitat. While such measures are not necessary from the lizard's point of view, if implemented with care, there is no reason not to decorate your pet's cage if you are inclined to do so.

However, it is recommended that beginners use a simple cage design for their first 6 to 12 months while they learn to provide effective husbandry.

Hide Boxes

"Hide boxes" come in a wide variety of shapes, sizes and styles. Some keepers use modified plastic or cardboard containers, while others use realistic looking logs and wood pieces. Both approaches are acceptable, but all hides must offer a few key things:

- Hides should be safe for the lizard and feature no sharp edges or toxic chemicals.

- Hides should accommodate the lizard, but not much else. They should be only slightly larger than the animal's body.

- Hides should have low profiles. Reptiles prefer to feel the top of the hide contacting the dorsal surface of their body.

- Hides either must be easy and economical to replace or constructed from materials that are easy to clean.

Plastic Storage Boxes
Just as a plastic storage box can be converted into an acceptable enclosure, small storage boxes can be converted into functional hiding places. Food containers, shoeboxes and butter tubs can serve as the base.

If the container has a low profile, it needs only have a door cut into the tub. Alternatively, you can discard the lid, flip the tub upside down and cut an entrance hole in the side.

Plant Saucers
The saucers designed to collect the water that overfills potted plants make excellent hiding locations. All you have to do is flip them upside down and cut a small opening in the side for a door.

Clay or plastic saucers can be used, but clay saucers are hard to cut. If you punch an entrance hole into a clay saucer, you must sand or grind down the edges to prevent hurting your pet.

Plates
Plastic, paper or ceramic plates make good hiding locations in cages that use particulate substrates. This will allow the lizard to burrow up under the plate through the substrate and hide in a very tight space. Such hiding places also make it very easy to access your pet while he is hiding.

Cardboard Boxes
While you must discard and replace them anytime they become soiled, small cardboard boxes can also make suitable hide boxes. Just cut a hole in the side to provide a door.

Commercial "Half-Logs"
Many pet stores sell U-shaped pieces of wood that resemble half of a hollow log. While these are sometimes attractive

looking items, they are not appropriate hide spots when used as intended.

The U-shaped construction means that the lizard will not feel the top of the hide when he is laying inside. These hides can be functional if they are partially buried, thus reducing the height of the hide.

Cork Bark
Real bark cut from the cork oak (*Quercus suber*), "cork bark" is a wonderful looking decorative item that can be implemented in a variety of ways.

Usually, cork bark is available in tube shape or in flat sheets. Flat pieces are better for blue-tongued skinks. Flat pieces should only be used with particulate, rather than sheet-like substrates so that the lizard can get under them easily.

Cork bark may be slightly difficult to clean, as its surface contains numerous indentations and crevices. Use hot water, soap and a sturdy brush to clean the pieces.

Commercially Produced Plastic Hides
Many different manufacturers market simple, plastic, hiding boxes. These are very functional if sized correctly, although some brands tend to be too tall. The simple design and plastic construction make them very easy to clean.

Paper Towel Tubes
Small sections of paper towel tubes make suitable hiding spots for young blue-tongued skinks. They do not last very long, so they require frequent replacement. They often work best if flattened slightly.

A blue-tongued skink basking on a rock.

Newspaper or Paper Towels

Several sheets of newspaper or paper towels placed on top of the substrate (whether sheet-like or particulate) make suitable hiding spots.

Many professional breeders use paper-hiding spaces because it is such a simple and economically feasible solution. Some keepers crumple a few of the sheets to give the stack of paper more height.

Unusual Items

Some keepers like to express their individuality by using unique or unusual items as hiding spots. Some have used handmade ceramic items, while others have used skulls or turtle shells. If the four primary criteria previously discussed are met, there is no reason such items will not make suitable hiding spaces.

Humid Hides

In addition to security, blue-tongued skinks also derive another benefit from many of their hiding spaces in the wild. Most hiding places feature higher humidity than the surrounding air.

By spending a lot of time in such places, blue-tongued skinks are able to avoid dehydration in habitats where water is scarce. Additionally, sleeping in these humid retreats aids in the shedding process. You should take steps to provide similar opportunities in captivity.

Humid hides can be made by placing damp sphagnum moss in a plastic container. The moss should not be saturated, but merely damp. You can also use damp paper towels or newspaper to increase the humidity of a hide box.

Some keepers prefer to keep humid hides in the habitat at all times, while others use them periodically – usually preceding shed cycles. Humid hides should never be the only hides available to the lizard. Always use them in addition to dry hides.

Chapter 10: Substrates

Substrates are used to give your blue-tongued skink a comfortable surface on which to crawl and to absorb any liquids present.

There are a variety of acceptable choices, all of which have benefits and drawbacks. The only common substrate that is never acceptable is cedar shavings, which emits fumes that are toxic to reptiles.

Paper Products

The easiest and safest substrates for blue-tongued skinks are paper products in sheet form. While regular newspaper is the most common choice, some keepers prefer paper towels, unprinted newspaper, butcher's paper or a commercial version of these products.

Paper substrates are very easy to maintain, but they do not last very long and must be completely replaced when they are soiled. Accordingly, they must be changed regularly -- at least once per week, and often every day.

Use several layers of paper products to provide sufficient absorbency and a little bit of cushion for the lizard.

Many pet stores and pet supply retailers now carry recycled paper pulp products that can be used as bedding. Many keepers have used these substrates successfully, but they don't offer the primary benefits that sheet-style paper products do.

For example, they're not as easy to replace and they represent an ingestion hazard. They also cost significantly more than a few sheets of newspaper, so they haven't become as popular as some keepers predicted.

Pine

Some hobbyists eschew pine, which is sometimes though to produce irritating fumes. While this may be true of products made from the xylem (wood) of pine trees, it is not true of products made from the bark.

Pine bark is not very absorbent, but it resists decay reasonably well. Pine bark is attractive and natural looking, but it does leave copious amounts of black dust inside the cage.

It can be spot cleaned daily but requires monthly replacement.

Orchid Bark

The bark of fir trees is often used for orchid propagation, and so it is often called "orchid bark." Orchid bark is very attractive, though not quite as natural looking as pine bark. However, it exceeds pine in most other ways except cost.

Because orchid bark is often reddish in color, it is very easy to spot clean. However, monthly replacement can be expensive for those living in the eastern United States and Europe.

Cypress Mulch

Cypress mulch is a popular substrate choice for many tropical species, and it helps to provide a high humidity level, which is often beneficial for blue-tongued skinks.

One significant drawback to cypress mulch is that some brands (or individual bags among otherwise good brands) produce a stick-like mulch, rather than mulch composed of thicker pieces.

These sharp sticks can injure the keeper and the kept. It usually only takes one cypress mulch splinter jammed under a keeper's fingernail to cause them to switch substrates.

Soil

Organic potting soil or soil collected from a forested area can also be used in your blue-tongued skink's enclosure. Both substrates are easy to acquire, affordable (or free) and retain moisture well, so they make excellent options.

Just be sure to collect the soil from an area that hasn't been exposed to pesticides or other chemicals, or, if you are purchasing the soil, opt for a variety that does not include perlite, fertilizers or other additives.

Chapter 11: Maintaining the Captive Habitat

Now that you have acquired your blue-tongued skink and set up the enclosure, you must develop a protocol for maintaining his habitat. While blue-tongued skink habitats require major maintenance every month or so, they only require minor daily maintenance.

In addition to designing a husbandry protocol, you must embrace a record-keeping system to track your blue-tongued skink's growth and health.

Cleaning and Maintenance Procedures

Once you have decided on the proper enclosure for your pet, you must keep your blue-tongued skink fed, hydrated and ensure that the habitat stays in proper working order to keep your captive healthy and comfortable.

Some tasks must be completed each day, while others are should be performed weekly, monthly or annually.

Daily
- Monitor the ambient and surface temperatures of the habitat.

- Spot clean the cage to remove any feces, urates or pieces of shed skin in the enclosure.

- Ensure that the lights, latches and other moving parts are in working order.

- Verify that your pet is acting normally and appears healthy. You do not necessarily need to handle him to do so.

Weekly
- Change sheet-like substrates (newspaper, paper towels, etc.).

- Clean the inside surfaces of the enclosure.

- Inspect your blue-tongued skink closely for any signs of injury, parasites or illness.

- Wash and sterilize all food dishes.

Monthly
- Break down the cage completely, remove and discard particulate substrates.

- Sterilize drip containers and similar equipment in a mild bleach solution.

- Measure and weigh your blue-tongued skink.

- Photograph your pet (recommended, but not imperative).

- Prune any plants present in the enclosure as necessary.

Annually
- Replace the batteries in your thermometers and any other devices that use them.

Cleaning your blue-tongued skink's cage and furniture is relatively simple. Regardless of the way it became soiled, the basic process remains the same:

1. Rinse the object
2. Using a scrub brush or sponge and soapy water, remove any organic debris from the object.
3. Rinse the object thoroughly.
4. Disinfect the object.
5. Re-rinse the object.
6. Dry the object.

Chemicals & Tools

A variety of chemicals and tools are necessary for reptile care. Save yourself some time by purchasing dedicated cleaning products and keeping them in the same place that you keep your tools.

Spray Bottles
Occasionally misting your pet's cage will help ensure the enclosure doesn't become too dry. You can do this with a small, handheld misting bottle or a larger, pressurized unit (such as those used to spray herbicides). Automated units are available, but they are rarely cost-effective unless you are caring for a large colony of animals.

Small Brooms
Small brooms are great for sweeping up small messes and bits of substrate. It is usually helpful to select one that features angled bristles, as they'll allow you to better reach the nooks and crannies of your pet's cage and the surrounding area.

Ideally, the broom should come with its own dustpan to collect debris, but there are plenty of workarounds for those that don't come with their own.

Scrub Brushes or Sponges
It helps to have a few different types of scrub brushes and sponges on hand for scrubbing and cleaning different items. Use the least abrasive sponge or brush suitable for the task to prevent wearing out cage items prematurely. Do not use abrasive materials on glass or acrylic surfaces. Steel-bristled brushes work well for scrubbing coarse, wooden items, such as branches.

Spatulas and Putty Knives
Spatulas, putty knives and similar tools are often helpful for cleaning reptile cages. For example, urates (which are not soluble in anything short of hot lava) often become stuck on cage walls or furniture. Instead of trying to dissolve them

with harsh chemicals, just scrape them away with a sturdy plastic putty knife.

Small Vacuums

Small, handheld vacuums are very helpful for sucking up the dust left behind from substrates. They are also helpful for cleaning the cracks and crevices around the cage doors. A shop vacuum, with suitable hoses and attachments, can also be helpful if you have enough room to store it.

Soap

Use a gentle, non-scented dish soap. Antibacterial soap is preferred, but not necessary. Most people use far more soap than is necessary -- a few drops mixed with a quantity of water is usually sufficient to help remove surface pollutants.

Bleach

Bleach (diluted to one-half cup per gallon of water) makes an excellent disinfectant. Be careful not to spill any on clothing, carpets or furniture, as it is likely to discolor the objects.

Always be sure to rinse objects thoroughly after using bleach and be sure that you cannot detect any residual odor. Bleach does not work as a disinfectant when in contact with organic substances; accordingly, items must be cleaned before you can disinfect them.

Veterinarian Approved Disinfectant

Many commercial products are available that are designed to be safe for their pets. Consult with your veterinarian about the best product for your situation, its method of use and its proper dilution.

Avoid Phenols

Always avoid cleaners that contain phenols, as they are extremely toxic to some reptiles. In general, do not use household cleaning products to avoid exposing your pet to toxic chemicals.

Keeping Records

It is important to keep records regarding your pet's health, growth and feeding, as well as any other important details. In the past, reptile keepers would do so on small index cards or in a notebook. In the modern world, technological solutions may be easier.

You can record as much information about your pet as you like, and the more information you record, the better. But minimally, you should record the following:

Pedigree and Origin Information
Be sure to record the source of your blue-tongued skink, the date on which you acquired him and any other data that is available. Breeders will often provide customers with information regarding the sire, dam, date of birth, weights and feeding records, but other sources will rarely offer comparable data.

Feeding Information
Record the date of each feeding, as well as the type of food item(s) offered. It is also helpful to record any preferences you may observe or any meals that are refused.

Weights and Length
Because you look at your pet frequently, it is difficult to appreciate how quickly he is (or isn't) growing. Accordingly, it is important to track his size diligently.

Weigh your pet with a high-quality digital scale. It is often easiest to use a dedicated "weighing container" with a known weight to measure your pet. Simply subtract the weight of the container to obtain the weight of your pet.

You can also measure your lizard's length as well, but it is not always easy to do so, as they tend to wiggle quite a bit. This can make it difficult to keep them in a straight line without putting undue pressure on their body.

However, there are a number of web-based computer applications that will calculate the length of snakes and lizards if you take and upload a photo of your pet along with something of a known length (such as a ruler).

Maintenance Information
Record all of the noteworthy events associated with your pet's care. While it is not necessary to note that you misted the cage every other day, it is appropriate to record the dates on which you changed the substrate or sterilized the cage.

Whenever you purchase new equipment, supplies or caging, note the date and source. This not only helps to remind you when you purchased the items, but it may help you track down a source for the items in the future, if necessary.

Breeding Information
If you intend to breed your blue-tongued skinks, you should record all details associated with pre-breeding conditioning, cycling, introductions, matings, color changes, copulations and parturition.

Record all pertinent information about any resulting litters as well, including the number of viable offspring, as well as the number of unfertilized ova (colloquially called "slugs" by keepers).

Chapter 12: Feeding Blue-Tongued Skinks

Blue-tongued skinks are omnivorous reptiles, who primarily feed on invertebrates, small vertebrates and vegetation.

The best diet for captive blue-tongued skinks is one that mimics their wild diet, being primarily comprised of gut-loaded insects, supplemented with plenty of leafy green vegetables and a small amount of fruit.

It is not necessary to feed blue-tongued skinks any vertebrate prey, although some keepers offer the occasional mouse to mature animals.

Like most other species, blue-tongued skinks benefit from a varied diet, which helps to minimize the effects of dietary excess and vitamin and mineral deficiencies.

However, providing a varied diet is not always sufficient to avoid deficiencies, so it is wise to supplement some of your pet's food with additional vitamins and minerals.

Insects

Insects should form the bulk of the diet for blue-tongued skinks of all sizes. Crickets or roaches make a nice staple, while the other insects can be incorporated to add variety.

Some keepers supplement their captive's diet with wild caught insects, but discretion is advised, as such insects may be contaminated with pesticides or infested with parasites.

The following insects make suitable prey for blue-tongued skinks:

- Crickets
- Roaches

- Mealworms
- Giant mealworms
- Superworms
- Wax worms
- Grasshoppers

Other Invertebrates

Aside from insects, a number of invertebrates make suitable food sources for blue-tongued skinks. However, few are available commercially, so they rarely form more than a trivial portion of a captive lizard's diet.

A few examples of acceptable invertebrates include:

- Earthworms
- Snails
- Slugs
- Roly-polies
- Small spiders

Vertebrates

In the wild, blue-tongued skinks occasionally consume small lizards or snakes. While your blue-tongued skink will remain perfectly healthy without eating any vertebrate prey, it is probably not a problem to offer the occasional mouse to your pet. However, too many rodents will quickly cause your pet to become obese and suffer from serious health problems.

If you choose to offer rodents to your pet, offer pre-killed, rather than live, individuals, to avoid any suffering on the part of the rodent.

Neither lizards nor snakes should not be offered as prey, as they are likely to be infested with parasites, which they may transmit to your pet.

Prey Size

Mature blue-tongued skinks can easily handle and consume relatively large insects; adult crickets and large roaches are rarely a problem.

Juveniles, by contrast, are often too small to consume large insects. In fact, feeding large insects to small blue-tongued skinks can cause them to become impacted.

In some cases, this can be fatal. To avoid such eventualities, offer small lizards insects that are no longer than the distance between the lizard's eyes.

How to Offer Food

You can either offer insects by adding them to the enclosure, individually via forceps, or you can use a feeding cup, which will keep the insects contained. Hand feeding is laborious, but acceptable if you do not mind devoting this amount of time to your pet's daily feedings.

If you elect to use a feeding cup, you will need to select a cup that is tall enough to keep the insects contained, and yet short enough that the lizard can reach them via his tongue. Alternatively, if the mouth of the cup is wide enough to accommodate the lizard's body, you can arrange a perch that allows the lizard to get close enough to the insects to reach them.

You can allow insects to sit in the feeding cup for about 24 hours, but do not let them sit in here for any longer. Clean the feeding cup daily with soap and water and disinfect it periodically.

Feeding Quantity and Frequency

Offer mature blue-tongued skinks food about three times per week. Provide your pet with as many insects as he will eat in about 10 minutes.

Young blue-tongued skinks will benefit from slightly smaller, yet more frequent meals. Accordingly, feed young skinks as many insects as they will eat in about 5 minutes but provide them with meals every other day.

Always remove any uneaten insects after the allotted time to prevent them from harming your pet.

Fruits and Vegetables

Although blue-tongued skinks consume a significant quantity of insects and other invertebrates, vegetation plays an important role in their diets as well. In addition to being rich in vitamins and minerals, most plant material is full of water, which will help keep your pet hydrated.

Dark leafy greens are the best vegetables to offer your lizard. As with insects, you'll want to remove and replace and vegetables remaining after about 24 hours to prevent them from spoiling.

In addition to leafy greens, you can also provide your pet with a number of other fruits and vegetables (see chart). Fruits and vegetables should be cut into small pieces or grated, and placed on a plate.

A twice- or thrice-weekly offering of plant material is likely sufficient for your pet's health, but there is little downside to offering vegetables and fruits more often than this if your pet is interested. Young blue-tongued skinks may show less interest in vegetables than adults do, but continue to offer them to your pet to instill good eating habits.

Here are a few foods that you can offer to your lizard, which are widely agreed to be safe. Remember that your lizard is an individual, with his own unique preferences and favorites – he may like some and avoid others.

Always wash all fruits and vegetables before offering them to your pet, to help remove any waxes or pesticides.

- Collard greens

- Turnip greens

- Mustard greens

- Dandelions

- Grape leaves

- Hibiscus

- Roses

- Cilantro

- Parsley

- Endive

- Kale

- Broccoli

- Carrots

- Squash

- Zucchini

- Pumpkin

- Kiwi

- Strawberries

- Blueberries

- Blackberries

- Apples

- Pears

Always avoid feeding blue-tongued skinks (or any other reptile) toxic fruits or vegetables. This includes things like avocados and rhubarb, but it is also important to avoid feeding your lizard the pits, seeds or cores of cherries, peaches, apples, pears or other fruits that contain cyanide.

Vitamin and Mineral Supplements

Many keepers add commercially produced vitamin and mineral supplements to their lizard's food on a regular basis. In theory, these supplements help to correct dietary deficiencies and ensure that captive lizards get a balanced diet. In practice, things are not this simple.

While some vitamins and minerals are unlikely to build up to toxic levels, others may very well cause problems if provided in excess. This means that you cannot simply apply supplements to every meal – you must decide upon a sensible supplementation schedule.

Additionally, it can be difficult to ascertain exactly how much of the various vitamins and minerals you will be providing to your lizard, as most such products are sold as fine powders, designed to be sprinkled on feeder insects.

This is hardly a precise way to provide the proper dose to your lizard, and the potential for grossly over- or under-estimating the amount of supplement delivered is very real.

Because the age, sex and health of your pet all influence the amount of vitamins and minerals he requires, and each individual product has a unique composition, it is wise to consult your veterinarian before deciding upon a supplementation schedule.

However, most keepers provide vitamin supplementation once each week, and calcium supplementation several times per week.

Chapter 13: Providing Water to Your Blue-Tongued Skink

Like most other animals, blue-tongued skinks require drinking water to remain healthy. And while providing drinking water is a fairly straightforward task, there are a few things to keep in mind while doing so.

Providing Drinking Water

Unlike many other lizards who do not seem to recognize water unless it is moving, blue-tongued skinks readily drink standing water, so you'll want to provide your pet with a dish full of clean, fresh drinking water at all times.

While it is acceptable to offer your pet a bowl that will accommodate his entire body, it is not necessary. A 4- to 6-inch dish is big enough in most cases (although there is nothing wrong with providing a large water dish – just make sure you keep it clean). Be sure to avoid filling large containers too high, as they are apt to overflow if the lizard crawls into the bowl.

Be sure to check the water dish daily and ensure that the water is clean. Empty, wash and refill the water dish any time it becomes contaminated with substrate, shed skin, urates or feces.

Some keepers prefer to use dechlorinated or bottled water for their reptiles; however, untreated tap water is used by many keepers with no ill effects.

Maintaining Proper Habitat Humidity

Blue-tongued skinks require fairly humid enclosures to thrive. Generally speaking, you'll want to shoot for a relative humidity between 40% and 50% during the day (although species from especially dry or damp areas may require you to adjust the humidity level accordingly). The humidity level can be allowed to drop at night.

To maintain a high humidity level, you'll need to periodically add water to the habitat to replace that which is lost as the air in the habitat mingles with the air in the surrounding room.

You can do so in a number of ways, but the easiest way to do so is by misting the habitat every day with room-temperature water. Be sure to spray down the sides of the enclosure as well as the substrate when doing so.

Additionally, you can keep the humidity relatively high by incorporating moisture-retaining substrates in the habitat. This includes things like cypress mulch and moss.

You can also pour water into the substrate if you like, but you'll need to make sure you don't add too much. Otherwise, you may flood the bottom of the habitat, which can lead to bacterial and fungal growth.

Chapter 14: Interacting with Your Blue-Tongued Skink

Blue-tongued skinks are easy to handle, and most captive individuals will learn to tolerate occasional interactions with their keeper.

In fact, it will occasionally be necessary to handle your pet to move him or inspect his health. Accordingly, you'll need to learn the best ways to do so.

Handling a Blue-Tongued Skink

The very best way to handle your blue-tongued skink is to allow him to walk on your outstretched hands, rather than physically restraining him. However, you may need to grip him gently but tightly, if you need to examine him closely.

To pick up your pet, try to slide a finger (or your entire hand, if the individual is large) underneath the lizard's chin. Gently apply upward pressure, and the lizard will usually begin moving up your hand or finger. Keep lifting up gently and the lizard may crawl right into your hand voluntarily.

Always be patient when transferring a blue-tongued skink to or from your hands. Try to "encourage" rather than "force" movements. Sometimes, tickling your lizard's foot or tail lightly will stimulate them to move more quickly.

In the Event of a Bite

Blue-tongued skink bites are somewhat rare, but they can cause some pain and they may break the skin. Accordingly, you should be prepared for the possibility, and understand the best course of action to take.

In the event of a bite, try to remain calm. If he does not release his bite quickly, you can simply move him into his habitat, and place his feet on the ground – he'll usually let go once he feels that he can escape.

If that doesn't work, you can try placing your hand under some cool, running water, which will normally cause him to let go.

Wash all bites with soap and warm water and consult your doctor if the bite breaks the skin.

Transporting Your Pet

Although you should strive to avoid any unnecessary travel with your lizard, circumstances often demand that you do (such as when your lizard becomes ill).

Strive to make the journey as stress-free as possible for your pet. This means protecting him from physical harm, as well as blocking as much stressful stimuli as possible.

The best type of container to use when transporting your lizard is a plastic storage box. Add several ventilation holes to plastic containers to provide suitable ventilation.

Add a few paper towel tubes to the container so your pet can hide and feel secure while traveling. Place a few paper towels or some clean newspaper in the bottom of the box to absorb any fluids, should your lizard defecate or discharge urates.

Monitor your lizard regularly but avoid constantly opening the container to take a peak. Checking up on your pet once every half-hour or so is more than sufficient.

Pay special attention to the enclosure temperatures while traveling. Use your digital thermometer to monitor the air temperatures inside the transportation container. Try to keep the temperatures in the low-70s Fahrenheit (21 to 22 degrees Celsius) so that your pet will remain comfortable. Use the air-conditioning or heater in your vehicle as needed to keep the animal within this range.

Keep your skink's transportation container as stable as possible while traveling. Do not jostle your pet unnecessarily and always use a gentle touch when moving the container. Never leave the container unattended.

Because you cannot control the thermal environment, it is not wise to take your lizard with you on public transportation.

Blue-tongued skinks usually tolerate gentle handling.

Hygiene

Reptiles can carry *Salmonella* spp., *Escherichia coli* and several other zoonotic pathogens and parasites. Accordingly, it is imperative to use good hygiene practices when handling reptiles. Always wash your hands with soap and warm water each time you touch your pet, his habitat or the tools you use to care for him. Antibacterial soaps are preferred, but standard hand soap will suffice.

In addition to keeping your hands clean, you must also take steps to ensure your environment does not become contaminated with pathogens. In general, this means keeping your skink and any of the tools and equipment you use to maintain his habitat separated from your belongings.

Establish a safe place to prepare your pet's food, store equipment and clean his habitat. Make sure the place is far from places human food is prepared. Never wash cages or tools in kitchens or bathrooms that are used by humans. Always clean and sterilize any items that become contaminated by the germs from your blue-tongued skink or his habitat.

Chapter 15: Common Health Concerns

Like many other reptiles, blue-tongued skinks are hardy animals, who often remain healthy despite their keeper's mistakes. In fact, most illnesses that befall pet blue-tongued skinks result from improper husbandry, and are, therefore, entirely avoidable.

Nevertheless, like most other reptiles, blue-tongued skinks often fail to exhibit any symptoms that they are sick until they have reached an advanced state of illness. This means that prompt action is necessary at the first hint of a problem. Doing so provides your pet with the greatest chance of recovery.

While proper husbandry is solely in the domain of the keeper, and some minor injuries or illnesses can be treated at home, veterinary care is necessary for many health problems.

Finding a Suitable Vet

While any veterinarian – even one who specializes in dogs and cats – may be able to help you keep your pet happy, it is wise to find a veterinarian who specializes in treating reptiles. Such veterinarians are more likely to be familiar with your pet species and be familiar with the most current treatment standards for reptiles.

Some of the best places to begin your search for a reptile-oriented veterinarian include:

- Veterinary associations

- Local pet stores

- Local colleges and universities

It is always wise to develop a relationship with a qualified veterinarian before you need his or her services. This way, you will already know where to go in the event of an emergency, and your veterinarian will have developed some familiarity with your pet.

When to See the Vet

Most conscientious keepers will not hesitate to seek veterinary attention on behalf of their pet. However, veterinary care can be expensive for the keeper and stressful for the kept, so unnecessary visits are best avoided.

If you are in doubt, call or email your veterinarian and explain the problem. He or she can then advise you if the problem requires an office visit or not.

However, you must always seek prompt veterinary care if your pet exhibits any of the following signs or symptoms:

- Traumatic injuries, such as lacerations, burns, broken bones or puncture wounds

- Sores, ulcers, lumps or other deformations of the skin

- Intestinal disturbances that do not resolve within 48 hours

- Drastic changes in behavior

- Inability to give birth

Remember that reptiles are perfectly capable of feeling pain and suffering, so apply the golden rule: If you would appreciate medical care for an injury or illness, it is likely that your pet does as well.

Common Health Problems

The following are some of the most common health problems that afflict blue-tongued skinks. Be alert for any signs of the following maladies and take steps to remedy the problem.

Respiratory Infections

Respiratory infections are some of the most common illnesses that afflict blue-tongued skinks and other captive reptiles.

The most common symptoms of respiratory infections are discharges from the nose or mouth; however, lethargy, inappetence and behavioral changes (such as basking more often than normal) may also accompany respiratory infections.

Myriad causes can lead to this type of illness, including communicable pathogens, as well as, ubiquitous, yet normally harmless, pathogens, which opportunistically infect stressed animals.

Your blue-tongued skink may be able to fight off these infections without veterinary assistance, but it is wise to solicit your vet's opinion at the first sign of illness. Some respiratory infections can prove fatal and require immediate attention.

Your vet will likely obtain samples, send off the samples for laboratory testing and then interpret the results. Antibiotics or other medications may be prescribed to help your blue-tongued skink recover, and your veterinarian will likely encourage you to keep the pet's stress level low and ensure his enclosure temperatures are ideal.

In fact, it is usually a good idea to raise the temperature of the basking spot upon first suspecting that your blue-tongued skink is suffering from a respiratory infection. Elevated body temperatures (such as those that occur when mammals have fevers) help the pet's body to fight the infection, and many will bask for longer than normal when ill.

Internal Parasites

In the wild, most reptiles carry some internal parasites. While it may not be possible to keep a lizard completely free of internal parasites, it is important to keep these levels in check.

Consider any wild-caught skink to be parasitized until proven otherwise. While most captive bred lizards should have relatively few internal parasites, they can suffer from such problems as well.

Most internal parasites that are of importance for blue-tongued skinks are transmitted via the fecal-oral route. This means that eggs (or similar life stages) of the parasites are released with the feces. If the lizard inadvertently ingests these, the resulting parasites can develop inside the lizard's body and cause illness.

Such eggs are usually microscopic and easily lifted into the air, where they may stick to cage walls or land in the water dish. Later, when the lizard flicks its tongue or drinks from the water dish, it ingests the eggs.

Because cages that are continuously contaminated from feces are likely to lead to dangerous parasite loads, employ strict hygiene practices at all times.

Internal parasites may cause your pet to vomit, pass loose stools, fail to grow or refuse food entirely. Other parasites may produce no symptoms at all, which illustrates the importance of routine examinations.

Your veterinarian will usually examine your lizard's feces if he suspects internal parasites. By looking at the type of eggs inside the lizard's feces, your veterinarian can determine which medication will treat the problem.

Many parasites are easily treated with anti-parasitic medications, but often, these medications must be given several times to eradicate the pathogens completely.

Some parasites may be transmissible to people, so always take proper precautions, including regular hand washing and keeping reptiles and their cages away from kitchens and other areas where foods are prepared.

Examples of common internal parasites include roundworms, tapeworms and amoebas.

External Parasites

The primary external parasites that afflict lizards are ticks and snake mites. Ticks are rare on captive bred animals, but wild caught reptiles may be plagued by dozens of the small arachnids. In fact, ticks are especially common on wild-caught blue-tongued skinks.

Ticks should be removed manually. Using tweezers grasp the tick as close as possible to the skink's skin and pull with steady, gentle pressure. Do not place anything over the tick first, such as petroleum jelly, or carry out any other "home remedies," such as burning the tick with a match. Such techniques may cause the tick to inject more saliva (which may contain diseases or bacteria) into your pet's body.

Drop the tick in a jar of isopropyl alcohol to kill it. It is a good idea to bring these to your veterinarian for analysis. Do not contact ticks with your bare hands, as many species can transmit disease to humans.

Mites are another matter entirely. While ticks are generally large enough to see easily, mites are about the size of a pepper flake. Whereas very bad tick infestations number in the dozens, mite infestations may include thousands of individual parasites.

Mites may afflict wild caught lizards, but, as they are not confined to a small cage, such infestations are somewhat self-limiting. In captivity, mite infestations can approach plague proportions.

After a female mite feeds on a lizard (or snake), she drops off and finds a safe place (such as a tiny crack in a cage or among the substrate) to deposit her eggs. After the eggs hatch, they travel back to your pet (or to other reptiles in your collection) where they feed and perpetuate the lifecycle.

Whereas a few mites may represent little more than an inconvenience to the lizard, significant infestations can stress them considerably. In extreme cases, they may even lead to anemia and eventual death. This is particularly true for small or young animals. Additionally, mites may transmit disease from one reptile to another.

There are a number of different methods for eradicating a mite infestation. In each case, there are two primary steps that must be taken: You must eradicate the lizard's parasites and eradicate the parasites in the environment (which includes the room in which the cage resides).

It is relatively simple to remove mites from a reptile. When mites get wet, they die. However, mites are protected by a thick, waxy exoskeleton that stimulates the formation of an air bubble.

To defeat this waxy cuticle, you can simply add a few drops of liquid soap to the water. The soap will lower the surface tension of water, thereby preventing the air bubble from forming.

Soaking your lizard is the slightly soapy water for about one hour will kill most of the mites on his body. Use care when doing so but try to arrange the water level and container so that most of the skink's body is below the water.

While your pet is soaking, perform a thorough cage cleaning. Remove everything from the cage, including water dishes, substrates and cage props. Sterilize all impermeable cage items and discard the substrate and all porous cage props. Vacuum the area around the cage and wipe down all of the nearby surfaces with a wet cloth.

It may be necessary to repeat this process several times to eradicate the mites completely. Accordingly, the very best strategy is to avoid contracting mites in the first place. This is why it is important to purchase your reptile from a reliable breeder or retailer and keep it quarantined from potential mite vectors.

Even if you purchase your lizard from a reliable source, provide excellent husbandry and clean the cage regularly, you can end up battling mites if your friend brings his snake or lizard – which has a few mites – to your house.

It may even be possible for mites to crawl onto your hands or clothes, hop off when you return home and make their way to your pet.

Make it a practice to inspect your lizard and his cage regularly. Look in the crease under the animal's lower jaw, near the eyes and near the vent -- common places in which mites hide. It can also be helpful to wipe down your skink with a damp, white paper towel. After wiping down the animal, observe the towel to see if any mites are present.

Chemical treatments are also available to combat mites, but you must be very careful with such substances. Beginners should rely on their veterinarian to prescribe or suggest the appropriate products to use.

Avoid repurposing lice treatments or other chemicals, as is often encouraged by other hobbyists. Such non-intended use may be very dangerous, and it is often in violation of federal laws.

New hobbyists should consult with their veterinarian if they suspect that their pet has mites. Mite eradication is often a challenging ordeal that your veterinarian can help make easier.

"Mouth Rot"
Mouth rot – properly called stomatitis – can be identified by noting discoloration, discharge or cheesy-looking material in your blue-tongued skink's mouth. Mouth rot can be a serious illness and requires the attention of your veterinarian.

While mouth rot often follows injury (such as happens when a lizard runs into the side of a glass cage) it can also arise from systemic illness. Your veterinarian will cleanse your pet's mouth and potentially prescribe an antibiotic.

Your veterinarian may recommend withholding food until the problem is remedied. Always be sure that lizards that are recovering from mouth rot are kept in immaculately clean habitats with ideal temperature gradients.

Injuries

Blue-tongued skinks can become injured in myriad ways. While they are likely to heal from most minor wounds without medical attention, serious wounds will necessitate veterinary assistance.

Your vet will likely clean the wound, make any repairs necessary and prescribe a course of antibiotics to help prevent infection. Be sure to keep the enclosure as clean as possible during the healing process.

Prolapse

Prolapses occur when a blue-tongued skink's intestines protrude from its vent. This is an emergency situation that requires prompt treatment. Fortunately, intestinal prolapse is not terribly common among blue-tongued skinks.

You will need to take the animal to the veterinarian, who will attempt to re-insert the intestinal sections. Sometimes sutures will be necessary to keep the intestines in place while the muscles regain their tone.

Try to keep the exposed tissue damp, clean and protected while traveling to the vet. It is likely that this problem is very painful for the animal, so try to keep its stress level low during the process.

Quarantine

Quarantine is the practice of isolating animals to prevent them from transferring diseases between themselves.

If you have no other pet reptiles (particularly other blue-tongued skinks), quarantine is unnecessary. However, if you already maintain other blue-tongued skinks you must provide all new acquisitions with a separate enclosure.

At a minimum, quarantine all new acquisitions for 30 days. However, it is wiser still to extend the quarantine period for 60 to 90 days, to give yourself a better chance of discovering any illness present before exposing your colony to new, potentially sick, animals. Professional zoological institutions often quarantine animals for six months to a year. In fact, some zoos keep their animals in a state of perpetual quarantine.

Chapter 16: Breeding Blue-Tongued Skinks

Many reptile keepers are intrigued at the idea of breeding their pets. While this is a fun, educational activity, you must be sure that you understand the risks and responsibilities that accompany such attempts.

For example, males may suffer damaged hemipenes and females may become egg bound. Either of which may be fatal without prompt treatment. You may find it necessary to take your pet to the veterinarian for costly treatment – often without any guarantee of success.

If you manage to get through the entire process without difficulty, you will one day find young blue-tongued skinks exploring the habitat and in need of care. While it is possible to sell them, this is not as easy as it sounds, and rarely generates profit.

Many municipalities require expensive permits to keep large numbers of reptiles – selling them requires other permits altogether. You will have to learn how to ship blue-tongued skinks and obtain the necessary permits for that.

Additionally, you will have to spend money to advertise that you have lizards for sale. Ultimately, most beginners find that it is simply best to give away their blue-tongued skinks to other keepers.

Finally, you must consider the costs associated with housing a large number of neonates. Each will need its own food supply and enclosure.

Pre-Cycling Conditioning

Only blue-tongued skinks in perfect health should be considered for breeding trials. If a lizard exhibits signs of stress, respiratory illness, mites, mouth rot or other illnesses, avoid breeding the animal until it is 100 percent health.

Prior to the breeding season, you'll need to feed adults slated for breeding trials heavily. However, avoid allowing either animal to become overweight – overweight blue-tongued skinks make poor breeders.

Cycling

Like many other reptiles, blue-tongued breed most reliably when cycled in a manner that mimics the seasonal changes in their native lands.

However, this may not always be necessary to trigger reproduction, and it is probably more important for those species and subspecies that live in areas with greater seasonal variation. This primarily means those species living in central and southern Australia.

The northern portions of Australia and New Guinea do not experience drastic differences in temperature throughout the year. Rainfall amounts, however, may vary considerably over the course of the year.

This rainy season occurs in the summer for most parts of Australia, so it is wise to allow the habitat to dry slightly while preparing to introduce the lizards to each other.

Pairing

Most keepers maintain blue-tongued skinks separately throughout the year and only pair them when attempting to stimulate breeding behavior.

Always observe blue-tongued skinks carefully when you introduce them to each other – particularly when it is the first time two have met. Some lizards just are not compatible, and they may engage in antagonistic behaviors or fight. This can lead to serious injuries or death if the subordinate animal cannot escape.

Some breeders prefer to place males in the females' cages, while others prefer the opposite. Still others use a neutral cage, unique to both. Introducing the male to the female's enclosure is probably the most natural strategy.

Pairs may begin copulating minutes after you place them in the same cage, or they may never breed if they are not compatible. Generally, you'll want to place your blue-tongued skinks together for several weeks to ensure the best chances of fertile matings.

Note that breeding is not a gentle affair for blue-tongued skinks. Males typically chase the females and bite them on the head, neck or back. Minor wounds are common, but be ready to intervene if it appears as though the female's health or well-being is in jeopardy.

Parturition and Post-Partum Care

After several weeks of cohabitation, the male and female can be separated. You'll want to feed her heavily to help prepare her for the rigors of gestation and parturition. However, you must always offer smaller-than-normal food items at this time, to reduce the chances of disrupting the reproductive processes. It's also important to ensure that her basking spot is providing proper temperatures, so she can raise her body temperature adequately.

Most blue-tongued skinks will give birth about 100 days after successful mating takes place. They may do so at any hour of the day, so be sure to monitor gravid females closely as she approaches parturition.

Once the young are born, you'll want to separate them and move them to their nursery enclosures (more on this below).

Allow the female to rest and rehydrate for about 24 hours, and then offer her food. Most females eat ravenously at this time to help replenish their energy stores.

Hatchling Husbandry

Establish "nursery enclosures" for the young blue-tongued skinks about a week before you expect them to be born. The container should contain only a paper towel substrate, a very shallow water dish and a few places to hide (crumpled newspaper works well).

Keep the nursery very clean, slightly humid and at about 80 degrees Fahrenheit (26 degrees Celsius), 24-hours a day. You can begin offering food within a few days of their birth.

The hatchlings do not need much light – that coming in the side of the nursery is ample. Try not to handle the hatchlings until they are about one month old and eating well.

It is not uncommon for hatchlings to be born while still inside their amniotic sac. This is normal, and usually no cause for concern. The young will break free in short order, and they'll often eat the sac. If any of the young appear to be struggling to escape, it may help to spray the sac with warm water.

Young blue-tongued skinks are usually ready to be placed in their permanent enclosures within a few weeks. At this point, you can place them in habitats that are like small versions of the adult cages.

Chapter 17: Further Reading

Never stop learning more about your new pet's natural history, biology and captive care. This is the only way to ensure that you are providing your new lizard with the highest quality of life possible.

It's always more fun to watch your blue-tongued skink than to read about him, but by accumulating more knowledge, you'll be better able to provide him with a high quality of life.

Books

Bookstores and online book retailers offer a treasure trove of information that will advance your quest for knowledge. While books represent an additional cost involved in reptile care, you can consider it an investment in your pet's well-being. Your local library may also carry some books about blue-tongued skinks, which you can borrow for no charge.

University libraries are a great place for finding old, obscure or academically oriented books about blue-tongued skinks. You may not be allowed to borrow these books if you are not a student, but you can view and read them at the library.

Herpetology: An Introductory Biology of Amphibians and Reptiles
By Laurie J. Vitt, Janalee P. Caldwell
Top of Form
Bottom of Form
Academic Press, 2013

Understanding Reptile Parasites: A Basic Manual for Herpetoculturists & Veterinarians
By Roger Klingenberg D.V.M.
Advanced Vivarium Systems, 1997

Infectious Diseases and Pathology of Reptiles: Color Atlas and Text
Elliott Jacobson
CRC Press

Designer Reptiles and Amphibians
Richard D. Bartlett, Patricia Bartlett
Barron's Educational Series

Magazines

Because magazines are typically published monthly or bi-monthly, they occasionally offer more up-to-date information than books do. Magazine articles are obviously not as comprehensive as books typically are, but they still have considerable value.

Reptiles Magazine
www.reptilesmagazine.com/
Covering reptiles commonly kept in captivity.

Practical Reptile Keeping
http://www.practicalreptilekeeping.co.uk/
Practical Reptile Keeping is a popular publication aimed at beginning and advanced hobbies. Topics include the care and maintenance of popular reptiles as well as information on wild reptiles.

Websites

The internet has made it much easier to find information about reptiles than it has ever been.

However, you must use discretion when deciding which websites to trust. While knowledgeable breeders, keepers and academics operate some websites, many who maintain reptile-oriented websites lack the same dedication to scientific rigor.

Anyone with a computer and internet connection can launch a website and say virtually anything they want about blue-tongued skinks. Accordingly, as with all other research, consider the source of the information before making any husbandry decisions.

Note: at the time of printing, all the websites below were working. As the internet changes rapidly, some sites might no longer be live when you read this book. That is, of course, out of our control.

The Reptile Report
www.thereptilereport.com/
The Reptile Report is a news-aggregating website that accumulates interesting stories and features about reptiles from around the world.

Kingsnake.com
www.kingsnake.com
After starting as a small website for gray-banded kingsnake enthusiasts, Kingsnake.com has become one of the largest reptile-oriented portals in the hobby. The site features classified advertisements, a breeder directory, message forums and other resources.

The Vivarium and Aquarium News

www.vivariumnews.com/

The online version of the former print publication, The Vivarium and Aquarium News provides in-depth coverage of different reptiles and amphibians in a captive and wild context.

Journals

Journals are the primary place professional scientists turn when they need to learn about blue-tongued skinks. While they may not make light reading, hobbyists stand to learn a great deal from journals.

Herpetologica

www.hljournals.org/

Published by The Herpetologists' League, Herpetologica, and its companion publication, Herpetological Monographs cover all aspects of reptile and amphibian research.

Journal of Herpetology

www.ssarherps.org/

Produced by the Society for the Study of Reptiles and Amphibians, the Journal of Herpetology is a peer-reviewed publication covering a variety of reptile-related topics.

Copeia

www.asihcopeiaonline.org/

Copeia is published by the American Society of Ichthyologists and Herpetologists. A peer-reviewed journal, Copeia covers all aspects of the biology of reptiles, amphibians and fish.

Nature

www.nature.com/

Although Nature covers all aspects of the natural world, many issues contain information that blue-tongued skink enthusiasts are sure to find interesting.

Supplies

You can obtain most of what you need to maintain blue-tongued skinks through your local pet store, big-box retailer or hardware store, but online retailers offer another option.

Just be sure that you consider the shipping costs for any purchase, to ensure you aren't "saving" yourself a few dollars on the product yet spending several more dollars to get the product delivered.

Big Apple Pet Supply
http://www.bigappleherp.com
Big Apple Pet Supply carries most common husbandry equipment, including heating devices, water dishes and substrates.

LLLReptile
http://www.lllreptile.com
LLL Reptile carries a wide variety of husbandry tools, heating devices, lighting products and more.

Doctors Foster and Smith
http://www.drsfostersmith.com
Foster and Smith is a veterinarian-owned retailer that supplies husbandry-related items to pet keepers.

Support Organizations

Sometimes, the best way to learn about blue-tongued skinks is to reach out to other keepers and breeders. Check out these organizations, and search for others in your geographic area.

The National Reptile & Amphibian Advisory Council

http://www.nraac.org/

The National Reptile & Amphibian Advisory Council seeks to educate the hobbyists, legislators and the public about reptile and amphibian related issues.

American Veterinary Medical Association

www.avma.org

The AVMA is a good place for Americans to turn if you are having trouble finding a suitable reptile veterinarian.

The World Veterinary Association

http://www.worldvet.org/

The World Veterinary Association is a good resource for finding suitable reptile veterinarians worldwide.

References

Almeida, M. L.-R.-F. (2006). Distribution of neuromuscular junctions in laryngeal and syringeal muscles in vertebrates.

Anderson, S. P. (2003). The Phylogenetic Definition of Reptilia. *Systematic Biology.*

AUSTIN, C. C. (2006). Checklist and Comments on the Terrestrial Reptile Fauna of Kau Wildlife Area, Papua New Guinea. *Herpetological Review.*

Baghurst, C. M. (1998). Home range overlap of mothers and their offspring in the sleepy lizard, Tiliqua rugosa. *Behavioral Ecology and Sociobiology.*

Baghurst, C. M. (1998). Social monogamy and extra-pair fertilization in an Australian lizard, Tiliqua rugosa. *Behavioral Ecology and Sociobiology.*

Bergmann, P. J. (2008). A phylogenetic and functional approach to the study of the evolution of body shape in lizards (Squamata). *University of Massachusetts Amherst.*

Bruce A. Young, N. M. (2013). Reptile Auditory Neuroethology: What Do Reptiles Do with Their Hearing? *Insights from Comparative Hearing Research.*

Bull, A. R. (2000). The impact of tick parasites on the behaviour of the lizard Tiliqua rugosa. *Oecologia.*

Bull, G. D. (2006). Movement patterns in the monogamous sleepy lizard (Tiliqua rugosa): effects of gender, drought, time of year and time of day. *Journal of Zoology.*

C. Michael Bull, A. M. (1991). Asynchronous Seasonal Activity of Male and Female Sleepy Lizards, Tiliqua rugosa. *Journal of Herpetology.*

C. Michael Bull, S. J. (1999). Relatedness and avoidance of inbreeding in the lizard, Tiliqua rugosa. *Behavioral Ecology and Sociobiology.*

C. Michael Bull, Y. P. (1993). Parturition in the Sleepy Lizard, Tiliqua rugosa. *Journal of Herpetology.*

C.BULL, A. R. (1996). Mother–offspring recognition in two Australian lizards,Tiliqua rugosaandEgernia stokesii. *Animal Behaviour.*

Freake, C. M. (1999). Home-range fidelity in the Australian sleepy lizard, Tiliqua rugosa. *Australian Journal of Zoology.*

Freake, M. J. (2001). Homing behaviour in the sleepy lizard (Tiliqua rugosa): the role of visual cues and the parietal eye. *Behavioral Ecology and Sociobiology.*

George A. Bartholomew, V. A. (1965). Oxygen Consumption, Thermal Conductance, and Heart Rate in the Australian Skink Tiliqua scincoides. *Copeia.*

Jennifer Koenig, R. S. (2001). The ecology of an Australian reptile icon: how do blue-tongued lizards (Tiliqua scincoides) survive in suburbia? *Wildlife Research.*

Jennifer Koenig, R. S. (2002). The Dangers of Life in the City: Patterns of Activity, Injury and Mortality in Suburban Lizards (Tiliqua scincoides). *Journal of Herpetology.*

K. Myhre, a. H. (1969). Behavioral regulation of internal temperature in the lizard Tiliqua scincoides. *American Journal of Physiology.*

Keith A. Christian, J. K. (2003). Energetics of bluetongue lizards (Tiliqua scincoides) in a seasonal tropical environment. *Oecologica*.

M. Cabanac, T. H. (1967). Tiliqua scincoides: Temperature-Sensitive Units in Lizard Brain. *Science*.

Pamula, C. M. (1996). Sexually dimorphic head sizes and reproductive success in the sleepy lizard Tiliqua rugosa. *Journal of Zoology*.

R. Michael Burger, W. H. (2007). Evaluation of UVB reduction by materials commonly used in reptile husbandry. *Zoo Biology*.

Warburg, M. (1965). The influence of ambient temperature and humidity on the body temperature and water loss from two Australian lizards, Tiliqua rugosa (Gray) (Scincidae) and Amphibolurus barbatus cuvier (Agamidae). *Australian Journal of Zoology*.

Wurst, G. C. (1976). The Occurrence of Parietal Eyes in Recent Lacertilia (Reptilia). *Journal of Herpetology*.

Printed in Great Britain
by Amazon